MONEY ISN'T

Everything

EVERYTHING

Is Money

A personalized approach to valuing and trading time, energy, relationships and money

TOM SHEPARD

Tom Shepard
701 US Route One
Suite 4
Yarmouth, ME 04096
www.tomshepardeverythingismoney.com

Designed by: Bookery
Written with: Ruby Peru

Ordering Information:

Quantity sales. Special discounts are available on quantity purchases by corporations, associations, and others. For details, contact the publisher at the address above.

Orders by U.S. trade bookstores and wholesalers. Please contact Tom Shepard:
Tel: (207) 847-4032; Fax: (207) 221-1117 or visit:

tomshepardeverythingismoney.com

Printed in the United States of America

ISBN: 979-8-9876993-3-1

Second Edition

Table of Contents

Thank you to my family and friends.
Most especially Susi, Sydney, Kira and Owen.
I love you guys more than you will ever know.
Thanks Mom and Dad for everything.

And Thank you to everyone that taught me just
a piece of what is in this book. Your stories inspire
me everyday to seek the truth behind the little
loyalties that get in the way of best efforts.

Be well

*We are most nearly
ourselves when we
achieve the seriousness
of the child at play*

HERACLITUS

I N THE BEGINNING SHE crawled into our bed and reminded us that GOD exists.

Several months later SHE arrived again and crept over to Susan's side of the bed. Susan opened one eye, looked at her and mumbled, "Syd, I'll give you a hundred dollars if you go back to bed."

Joyously and with an energy out of sync with the time of day, Syd responded, "How about two hundred?" More evidence that GOD's humor is exponential. Ha ha!

Syd's response was music to the ears of this financial advisor. It brought a smile to my face. In small, joyful moments like these, our kids have taught us so much about how life works. Susan wanted peace and quiet and was willing to pay for it, which caused Syd to suddenly recognize that her power to awaken her parents (or choose to refrain from doing so) was a tradeable commodity. This moment was a good example of the fact that the presence of children requires us to negotiate daily among the primary currencies of time, energy, $tuff, and relationships to get the kinds of lives we desire.

Money is no good unless you use it

SYDNEY MADISON SHEPARD

The healthiest lesson I can think to share in this book is how to recognize the patterns of health and wealth that I first noticed during those early days I spent raising kids who constantly made me redefine the meaning of currency. After all, children negotiate with their parents using more than just money, because money isn't everything, nor is money the only currency. In a way, practically every aspect of life can serve as a currency at one time or another. I think truly understanding life's many currencies, how we trade them, and how we can make better trades is crucial to living a better life. That's why I say,

"Money isn't everything ... Everything is Money." After all, sometimes, in our currency trades, we succeed beyond our wildest expectations, count the blessings, and celebrate the deposits. Other times, we fall behind, fail at our endeavors, or find faults in ourselves or others that drain our spirits. This causes us to withdraw currencies we never realized were tradeable from accounts we didn't even know existed.

In these pages, you will also find my observations about the patterns that are woven into nature and thus exist throughout our lives. These patterns exist in the smallest and largest structures in the universe. They are also discussed and preached about in all the world's major religions. Consider rainbows in the sky, ripples on a pond, waves in the ocean, musical notes scaling up, and snowflakes falling down. Because we can easily observe these patterns, we can believe in them, have faith in them, trust them, and use them to understand our beautiful world. This information from the heavens shows us how to build sustainably, embrace change, and celebrate birth and death, all while hinting at an existence beyond this present one. Yet, in our understanding of this world filled with patterns, blind spots arise that may frustrate us and distort our understanding of Earth and Heaven alike. This is why, when we learn to identify life's many currencies along with nature's intrinsic patterns, we can use these mysterious elements to improve our lives in agreement with the natural world.

When we are young, we embrace uncertainty and enjoy the partial truths of myths and legends. To us, life's magic is its mystery, and its mystery is magical. As we grow older, however, we lose our appreciation for the unknown and undefined. This becomes a flaw in our hardware and a supreme vulnerability. When children offer us the gift of love, they help us simultaneously accept imperfection and strive for improvement. They teach us that life's ups and downs, blacks and whites, can all be recognized without malice, the way a coin has both its head and tail sides as part of a greater whole, without quarrel. One can even find humor in these paradoxes.

While my wife and I were raising young kids at home, I was training young financial advisors, at work. Mostly in their twenties, these "children" needed to be able to speak with wisdom to clients in their forties through eighties. They came up with innumerable philosophies to conceal the fact that they were novices.

One philosophy was, "Fake it 'til you make it!"

Another was, "Don't think. You'll weaken the nation."

Then there were those who adhered to, "The law of large numbers."

Others said the answer was to: "Churn and burn."

But my philosophy, the one in this book, was different. I built it over time by trying to overcome the simplistic efficiency of what educators call "drill for skill," or rote memorization of facts. I was looking for a more professional and productive way not just to succeed in my field but to love and respect every lead. In this philosophy, there was no such thing as a good or bad lead (Glengarry anyone?). No such thing as a good or bad prospect. No such thing as a good or bad client. No such thing as a magical or perfect amount of activity. Instead, there was a pattern to identifying and helping adults get what they want out of life by using the stored and potential energy of money to unlock the value and flow of all their resources and talents.

As a result of this viewpoint, in our office, we discussed the four things everyone values—time, health, money, and relationships—as well as the dual nature of these desires. People want things either now or later, emphasize either quantity or quality, and seek to either protect or pursue. In talking about these dual desires, we discussed the financially motivated acts of spending, earning, saving, investing, borrowing, giving, and taking and how they contribute to, or detract from, the dichotomies above. As a result, over time, we observed a pattern in the combination of these elements. The pattern repeated but in a complex way, and in the end, a helical model arose.

In the larger world at this time, studies of behavioral economics were being published. Social scientists observed and wrote about personality types as useful tools for predicting success. Financial guru Tony Robbins put forth complex ideas having to do with money and personalities and human nature; meanwhile, something called "financial therapy" became a professional pursuit. These social changes resulted in a need for financial planners to get additional specialized training. To me, it soon seemed like there was an overabundance of philosophizing about the roles of "nature" versus "nurture" in terms of each individual's ability to manage money. In fact, I felt that the more we, as a society, valued the "nurture" story, the more difficult it was to stay in touch with the simpler building blocks of "nature," which, in my opinion, are far more important. In the financial philosophy of the day, it seemed like "deny thyself" was replacing "know thyself." With this new financial viewpoint, the Western Roman rule of law and recipe was gradually replacing the Eastern Greek ideas of flow and identity.

In my effort to educate the "children" as to the way they should go, I wanted to train talented chefs, not hire a bunch of cooks. They should know how to identify for themselves and others why each and every rock in the (financial planning) river was there and know its purpose. I wanted to see them craft a living in a new way—out of raw and abundant ingredients based on the seasons and stages of life. The evolutionary method in this book came out of those ideas and the notion of not "this versus that," but rather "this and that." This philosophy enables one to choose heads and tails instead of heads or tails, US instead of VS.

For me, the black and white mathematics of money helped me see difference, while the lens of all currency helped me split the white into vivid colors and work with them using a wider variety of operations. I used a sense of awareness and purpose for motivating and directing our actions, instead of simple, goal-directed behavior. As such, my "children" felt pulled instead of pushed. We all learned to let go and allowing the gravity of each client's situation do its own work to nudge the world toward reconnecting each client's nature and DNA with the primordial soup of currency in which it swims.

In the pages that follow, I hope you will feel inspired to read and browse and explore and experience what we have put down in words using the technique that works best for you. You can read the book in order, slowly. You can also browse it and focus more on the pictures. You can explore one section deeply or speed read the whole book, then go back to your favorite sections. You can even browse, glimpse, or stare at the pages just for the sheer experience of it. Underline, dog ear, highlight, rip out a section, or even take a photo of a picture. Use the book, because it's no good to anybody put on a shelf or stored in a safety deposit box. Like money, the ideas in this book have to flow. I hope they do that through you and perhaps even get modified in some way by interacting with you. I put this book out there as a good book that will only become great by interacting with you, the reader.

Kids of all ages grow up too fast. So, heed the wisdom of ancestors and little children.

Welcome, Explorer!

TALKING ABOUT MONEY sets some people on edge. For others, it's a fascinating topic that turns them into armchair philosophers. But these different attitudes don't necessarily come about relative to how much money or debt you have. In fact, in my twenty-seven years of experience as a financial planner, I find that peoples' attitudes about money—including their own financial self-assessments—are seldom based upon how much money or debt they actually have but upon their way of seeing the world in general. That's why this book is not exactly about managing money. It's about examining the ways we view our world, what we truly value as assets and resources, and how we're motivated to trade. It's also about making sure our behaviors are synchronized with our values. Altogether, it's about holistic financial planning, also known as "life planning."

I'd like you to see financial planning as not a chore but an adventure. In reading this book, many of you are, after all, heading off into an unknown

> *Whoever cannot seek the unforeseen sees nothing, for the known way is an impasse*
>
> HERACLITUS

world. Who knows, that world might contain treasures beyond your wildest dreams, but there are pitfalls, too.

When considering embarking on any adventure, I find it interesting to note that it's well known among outdoor enthusiasts that one reason people get lost in the woods is that without something to guide their way, they end up walking in a circle. Interestingly, some wander to the right and some to the left. Nobody quite knows why. Thinking you've made progress only to find yourself right back where you started is incredibly frustrating, but we've all experienced it in one way or another, haven't we? To avoid that fate out in the woods, you need certain instruments and skills to keep you on track. Dead reckoning (or pure instinct) is one such skill, but there are others you can learn. This is true for your financial journey as well. Let's use your resources to build a life that seamlessly integrates instinct, self-knowledge, and logic. With that in mind, this book is written in four parts.

The first part talks about your PURPOSE for taking this journey to begin with. We call that purpose "currency," but our lives consist of many currencies and what you'll learn in this book can help you with all of them, not just money.

The second part helps you find out more about your SELF and who you are before beginning your adventure. Each individual embarks upon a trek in a unique way. Some may have a longer gait, others take shorter steps. Some explore every side trail, others stick to the well-traveled path or bushwhack through the wilderness. Some explorers want to bring a lot of gear along, others chose to travel light. So, before embarking upon your journey, it's important to first know who you are—your individual strengths, weaknesses, and preferences.

> *I speak, that you may learn here-after never to rest in duties*
>
> THOMAS SHEPARD, HARVARD FOUNDING FATHER CIRCA 1642

The third part provides a MAP with a big X and a "You are here!" sign to show where you are right now, your destination options, and the waypoints along the path to each destination.

The fourth part of the system I'm about to teach you functions as a COMPASS. When you're lost in the woods, a tool like a compass can help you find your way by pointing you in the right direction. Similarly, this book provides an intellectual tool you'll learn that will always show you the way to the next stop along your journey, no matter what type of SELF you have, no matter what PURPOSE you seek.

The fifth thing every intrepid explorer needs is a GUIDEBOOK to help navigate the pitfalls and appreciate the wonders along the way. This book is that guidebook, and it contains a workbook section where you can customize what you've learned for your life and unique needs. That said, let's start our journey!!

PART 1

Purpose

It is in changing that
we find purpose

HERACLITUS

What is Currency?

LEGAL TENDER, BANK notes, scratch, Benjamins, bacon, bones, bread, big ones, bucks, C notes, cabbage, cheddar, cha-ching, clams, dead presidents, dough, greenbacks, lucre, loot, lettuce … When someone says "currency" most people think of cash, but currency can be anything we trade in a transaction. If you give one thing to get another, you're using those items as currency. When making any type of trade or expending any type of energy, you generally want something: That's your PURPOSE. In this book, the way we talk about your purpose in any endeavor is called "currency."

If you give up some of your free time to help a friend in need, that's a transaction where **time** and **friendship** are the currencies being traded. If you work all night without sleeping in order to impress a teacher with your incredible science fair project, you're trading your **health** for a **relationship.** Good **relationships** and friendships are hard to come by. So is good **health.** So is free time. We value all these currencies and think twice before giving them away. But when the trade is a good one, it's worth it.

Importantly, when you have surplus in one of the currencies, it's more likely to be worth doing a trade because there's less risk for you. Often, young people have a surplus in **health** and wellness while older folks might have more of a surplus in actual cash. While parents tend to have a deficit in time, they often enjoy surplus in their relationship currency.

Quite simply, financial planning is about managing a monetary surplus in order to increase it. To that end, this book asks two questions:

> ➤ *In which currency do you actually have a surplus?*

> ➤ *In which currency would you like to have more of a surplus?*

No matter which currency you seek to improve, you can use the principles in this book to trade up.

What makes a good trade? That's up to the needs of each individual, of course, so determining your unique needs and wants is the very first thing we do when we consider how to handle the currency in your life. Although there is no one-size-fits-all program for financial planning, this book provides a system that helps people determine their priorities and goals and predictably rise to the next level in what they value. I think you'll find the prospect a lot easier than you expect. That said, this book is also for those who are already adept at financial planning, because what I present here is a new (and I dare say simpler) way to find and immediately address your personal financial strengths and weaknesses.

The system, on its face, is easy to learn, but in order to have it change your life, it's important to internalize its deeper meaning. In that case, this mode of thinking sends tendrils out into all facets of your life, affecting the way you view every type of currency and helping you make improvements in non-financial areas as well. When it comes to holistic financial planning, "financial" is interpreted as "what you value" rather than being limited to just legal tender, bank notes, scratch, Benjamins, bacon, bones, and bread. This system is also sensitive to past traumas, helping you make progress without requiring you to relive mistakes or hold onto the past.

To that end, my system recognizes four different types of currency: **time, health, relationships,** and **stuff**. It's possible you're up against the wall in all those currencies, but if you have a little bit of surplus in even one of them, you're ready to take the next step.

What is Surplus?

Turning briefly to the Biblical story of Adam and Eve, you might recall that God put the pair in the Garden of Eden (where they had everything they needed for survival) and told them simply not to eat a certain apple. What did they do? They ate the apple, of course.

Some say the restriction around the apple was meant to test their obedience. After eating it, they suddenly wanted clothes, which they didn't need before. Some say this meant the apple made them aware of sin. But as a financial planner, I see the story differently. To me, the apple is clearly a symbol of surplus. Since the garden provided everything they needed without it, the apple represented something they wanted but didn't need. After eating this surplus item, Adam and Eve became aware of their ability to create, so they made clothes: another thing they wanted but didn't need, another form of surplus.

By the same token, if your kitchen garden produces too many tomatoes (stuff), you might cook them (energy) and can or jar (relationship) the sauce, which keeps longer (time) than fresh tomatoes. Now that you have time on your side, you can trade the sauce for different types of surplus such as clothes, tricycles, telescopes, therapy, medicine, or even a chef to cook meals for you. As such, your wealth will increase. If it's a good trade, so will the wealth of the person with whom you trade. Everybody wins!

The take-away here is that currency helps us achieve basic survival, but it takes on a different dimension when it becomes surplus. That's another level of currency. With surplus currency, you can improve your lifestyle much more efficiently. This book will teach you how.

Financial management is all about seeking ways to turn even the smallest amount of surplus into even more surplus until eventually you get bored of having so much surplus. At that point, for sheer amusement, you'll start from scratch again in one of the currencies just for the sheer challenge or fun of doing it all again.

"Going Back to a Simpler Time"

Keep in mind that with surplus comes complexity. The more you have, the more management you need to do in order to make your surplus work for you. If you know how to do this, it really improves your life, so it's worth the trouble. But if you don't know how to manage your surplus, it can cause you stress, instead. This is the point where you sometimes hear people say, "I'd like to go back to a simpler place and time!"

People in this phase fantasize about a vision of farm life or small-town life—anything without ambition—which seems easier for them. But what they are actually fantasizing about is the absence of surplus. In truth, farm life is very hard, and working without surplus can result in serious problems with your health and well-being, especially in the event of an emergency. So, "a simpler life" is not a panacea for anything. Learning how to best manage finances, including surplus, is the very thing that keeps any life feeling "simple," and that's why you and I are here together, today.

Anything you're responsible for but lack the skill to manage can cause stress. Think of adopting a dog. You have to train it, feed it, and give it plenty of exercise or else it could misbehave and cause you a lot of stress. A bad dog is a type of currency (relationship) that you haven't learned to manage. Let's not allow your finances to become bad dogs but make them into well-behaved, loving pets—especially the rescued ones!

The Four Currencies

For those readers already well-versed in the art of financial planning, this book is for you, but the rest of this chapter may not be, and you can skip ahead to chapter two. The next couple of pages are directed at my readers who, when forced to talk about money, do a little dance that kind of looks like a trapped animal retreating into a corner and screaming for its life. If that's you, I get you. Let's ease into the subject of that-which-shall-not-be-named.

When you get up in the morning, do you think about the events of the day ahead? Do you talk yourself out from under your cozy comforter by reminding yourself there's hot coffee waiting and a delicious breakfast? Then, do you contemplate the next steps: do this first, then that, then take care of these items. Now that you've faced what's ahead, isn't it easier to get up and start your day? That, of course, is what we call planning. You just planned your use of the currency of time. For many, habits often take the place of planning, and this book is meant to help you reassess the habits that aren't helping you.

On the other hand, perhaps you're a freelancer who decides each morning whether to work that day or go snowboarding. You make different decisions about time every single day, and you can't predict exactly what each day will hold. You're the type of person who doesn't like to plan your time. But in order to live this way, you need other resources. You need relationships with fun friends

The Four Currencies, Broadly

To keep things simple, I have only identified four types of currency (stuff, relationship, health, and time) but these are broad categories.

For instance, under stuff, you have money and everything you can buy with money. That's a lot!

Under relationship, you've got everything including parent, friend, spouse, friend-of-a-friend, second cousins, neighbors … the possibilities are too numerous to list.

Health includes mental health, physical well-being, and emotional stability.

Time is the least tangible but, in many ways, most easily measured currency. We quantify time with seconds, minutes, and hours as well as seasons and phases of the moon.

Surely, you value many things in life that aren't easily quantified, such as your reputation, world peace, and a clear conscience. The best way to maximize anything you value is to figure out under which of these four categories it exists. We do that by determining the measurements used to quantify that thing. (See additional sidebars for more.)

who like to go snowboarding. You need relationships with clients who are flexible about their due dates. Your life depends upon the building and management of relationships that enable you to live the way you like. You manage relationships in order to avoid managing time. In short, all people need to manage some type of resource to achieve their goals, and sometimes that resource isn't tangible.

Have you ever sold your old things at a garage sale, on Ebay, or Craigslist? Or bought groceries? Or splurged on the wedding of your dreams? That's management of what I call stuff. Money is important but only in-so-much-as it can buy the stuff you need, so money is a subset of the currency of stuff.

Finally, if you exercise control over the food you eat and your fitness level, if you psych yourself up for a big challenge by listening to your favorite music, or even if you drink coffee to give yourself more energy, you're actively managing the currency of health. If we're alive, we all have some level of health—mental, physical, and spiritual—and usually we wish for more. Health is the currency that gives us the energy we need to accomplish what we want to do in life.

Do you carpool? That's time management. Do you network for business? That's relationship management. Do you express gratitude when things go your way? That's health management. Do you enjoy a glass of wine in a pleasant atmosphere? When you decide how many glasses you'll drink, how often, at what price point—that's stuff management. In short, everybody manages something, whether they feel like "an organized person" or not. Everybody plans something, whether they feel like "a planner" or not. If you're an adult—and this is even true for many children—you have planned and managed some type of currency already. In fact, when it comes to your favorite currency (Milkshakes? Broadway shows? Llamas?) you're probably pretty good at it.

You are Already an Expert

Managing stuff can feel scary because of the emotional baggage we often attach to money. If your calculations show you to be living above your means, this can drop some people into depression. Conversely, if your calculations reveal that you have surplus income, people sometimes feel guilty, as if they have taken something deserved by another. Just the act of calculating monthly expenditures can send some people into a psychological tailspin because of all the emotions wrapped up in the earning and spending of money. Let's name a few: guilt, greed, anger, regret, joy, worry, self-loathing … Shall I go on? For some of us, we'd rather go hang-gliding off an Alpine summit than do that truly risky thing: sit at a desk with a calculator and list of bank statements. However, most folks don't feel that level of emotional stress when managing the currency of time.

Just like money, time is a limited resource, and we do our best with it. When an important event has to be postponed, it's typically disappointing but not a reason to tear your hair out. You resolve to manage time better next time and move forward. Managing relationships can also be stressful, but there, too, we know that we can repair or move on from bad ones. Remember that old adage: "There are other fish in the sea?" It's a way of urging people not to let relationships overwhelm them, emotionally. The expression suggests that you remain calm because below the surface lies abundance. It helps to take the same attitude toward money.

When you're ready for the nitty-gritty of financial management, calculate the numbers, but don't fall into the trap of feeling anything about them. After you learn what I have to teach you here, you'll see how the numbers you come up with are actually pretty predictable. You'll also know the next step to take to improve those numbers. Improving the situation is, of course, the whole point of financial planning and the whole point of the system I'll be teaching you here.

Starting Your Financial Journey

This book likens your financial planning experience to a journey through the wilderness. Here in part one, we'll gain a firm understanding of our PURPOSE for this adventure. This isn't a general lecture about where people start, but an opportunity to use insight to see where you, as an individual, start your financial journey. Believe it or not, you've been starting at the same place your whole life.

In part two, we consider your SELF, or who you really are, before undertaking your journey through the financial wilderness. After all, in order to plan your adventure, we need to know if you're the type of person who wants to bushwhack the whole way, take well-traveled paths to get there quickly, or amble along sightseeing as you go. Your personal preferences, tendencies, special abilities, and weaknesses must be considered before we decide on a path forward.

Spirituality

Many people of a spiritual bent are willing to trade time, stuff, and relationship energy for that ultimate goal of spiritual enlightenment, inner peace, and a sense of connection to something greater than oneself. Spirituality is talked about in terms of "energy." Spiritual energy is certainly different from the units used to quantify your blood pressure, but both measurements have to do with energy, so spirituality typically falls under the heading of health.

On the other hand, spiritual currency can exist under the umbrella of relationship, too, as it is truly a function of one's relationship to the world and the self. So, depending upon the situation, your spiritual growth can be thought of as a unit of either relationship or health.

Part three provides a MAP that puts a big X and a "you are here!" sign on your current financial situation. It also shows all the places you can go on your financial journey and in what order those locations must be visited. There is no obligation to take the path all the way to the summit of the mountain, but you might as well know what advantages the summit holds, just in case you choose to go there.

When you're lost in the woods, you can use a tool, such as a COMPASS, to find your way. Similarly, part four of this book provides an intellectual tool (called the Financial States) to help you find your way in the financial wilderness. This tool shows you exactly how to get from where you are to the destination of your choice. It helps you turn in the right direction and look ahead—not back.

Let's get started! When? Now!

How We Manipulate Currencies

MEET SINGLE MOM Jane Dylon, whose daughter failed to thrive in public school. But the little girl loved playing outdoors, so, after a great deal of research, Jane found a small school for "different" kids that took them outdoors every day and taught them all about the natural world. No more desks! The adventure school was expensive, and it also cost Jane a lot more than money.

With its location an hour from Jane's home, the school required Jane to cooperate with the other parents to carpool, even though the students came from all over the region. Her carpool days were busy ones where—between driving students to school, then driving them back home again—Jane was lucky to have a half hour to catch her breath before the sun set. This school seemed to be the only answer for her child, so Jane gave up her nine-to-five job and found something more flexible. Instead of buying new clothes, she learned to repair the old ones. She also gave up a lot of social experiences she would otherwise have and all the family vacations she could no longer afford. Any parents out there see themselves in Jane's story?

When it comes to your child, the only currency that matters is your relationship with her and her relationship with the world. To build that

What is Time?

Time is comprised of moments, which can be measured in minutes, hours, milliseconds, and so on. You only get stuff if you go out and buy it. Relationships only grow if nurtured. Health is always there in some form or another, but time "marches on." Time is the only currency you have to spend whether you like it or not. If it's always spent on work, people feel cheated of "free time." But if it's frittered away on useless activities, people feel they have "wasted time."

For parents, budgeting the currency of time puts us in conflict with our kids for one simple reason: unaware that their time on Earth is limited, children consider time free and limitless, thus not a currency at all. What's more, as parents, we want them to keep that beautiful innocence as long as possible. Conflicts arise because this means we're struggling to help children wisely manage a currency they don't even believe exists.

relationship, which would last a lifetime, Jane traded money, time, and relationships with others. In so doing, she gained mental health for her child and herself ... priceless. In the long run, those trades paid off. Her child eventually became more stable as a result of the private school experience, and Jane could finally return her to public school and thus rearrange family life in a way that improved some of the currencies (like time and money) that she had devalued in her previous quest for health and relationship.

Had anyone asked Jane about her financial status during those early, private-school years, she would have just looked at them funny and asked, "Money? What money?" But in the big picture, Jane prepared herself and her daughter for better long-term financial success by ensuring her family had a solid foundation in the other currencies. That's holistic financial planning.

Let's also meet Sandy Bridgewater, an heiress. She grew up in a mansion with all the material advantages one could ever imagine but never had money of her own. As she grew older, her needs were taken care of by parents who used their control over the family money to guide her toward a career she didn't enjoy and a pre-feminist lifestyle she didn't value. She wanted more autonomy but figured if she was going to take the family money, she had to do the family's bidding. Then, after she turned eighteen, something strange started happening.

Every year she was called to a meeting with the shareholders of the family business and asked to sign some papers she didn't understand. When she finally got answers to her questions, she learned she had a right to refrain from signing away her share of the business, her inheritance. She had a right to millions of dollars that she could own outright, but it would mean the dissolution of the family business and legacy. In the long run, she chose not to sign the papers. The family business had to be dissolved in order for her to cash out her inheritance. The family shunned her, she became a millionairess in her own right, and she never looked back at the people who had, for so long, lied and kept her in the dark.

Sandy traded those **relationships** for money and a life of total independence. Her **time** was her own and her **health** was the best that money could buy. For years, she struggled to build back the **relationships** in her life amid extensive criticism for what she had done. However, the value of different currencies is not fixed, as Sandy's detractors would have had her believe, but dependent upon each individual. This trade of currencies felt right for Sandy's situation.

Health

When it comes to **health**, we can measure our blood pressure, sugar levels, even brain wave activity. These give us ways to quantify something multi-faceted and complex in order to assess and improve it. The thing that draws all these different test results together is that they all measure a type of energy. Energy is the unit we use to quantify **health**. So, if you value any type of currency in your life and it's measured in units of energy, you can think of it as falling under the heading of **health**.

From there, let's visit Paul, a Yogi, who enjoyed a simple life of meditation, conscious eating, yogic disciplines, and inexpensive pleasures. A founding member of a cooperatively-owned yoga school, he taught several classes per day, had no significant savings, and owned no property. Paul wasn't ambitious. He didn't borrow from relatives. He saw the pursuit of money as an evil that caused many of the physiological problems for which his students needed his teachings. Financial planning was the furthest thing from his mind, as his spiritual discipline taught him to value **time, relationships,** and **health** above money and the things it could buy. Yet, one day in 2020, he joined his fellow yoga teachers in a meeting with a financial planner.

Relationship

We typically build (and destroy) **relationships** with the use of words. They say communication is crucial to any relationship. I say words are the very unit by which **relationships** are measured. So, if there is something in life you value highly, and it is made up of words, consider it **relationship** currency. Here are some popular examples:

INFORMATION: Since information is typically expressed in units of words, everything from schoolwork to street smarts falls under "**relationship.**" No matter what language you speak, words are the unit used to convey information.

STATUS: A bad rumor can destroy someone's status in the community; meanwhile, great Yelp reviews can increase a company's status in the marketplace—all with the use of words. This currency sometimes also overlaps with **stuff**, because money can bring status and vice versa.

Coronavirus had suddenly shut down the yoga cooperative. For the first time, the need for security raised its head among the yogis. This made Paul acknowledge that he needed to make money part of his spiritual practice. Just like the way he did his yoga, Paul set an intention for his meeting with the financial planner, and, as he learned more and more about money management, he checked in with himself, just as one does in a yoga pose, asking,

"Does this feel right?"

"Is anything misaligned?"

"Am I pushing myself too hard?"

"Can I go deeper and achieve more?"

He breathed deeply through the learning process and caught himself whenever he felt an impulse to panic or judge himself.

Sadly, the financial planner was unable to save the cooperative, so Paul needed to make a big change in his financial life. To that end, he found a stopgap job in the community. It wasn't in his field, and he didn't love it, but it paid enough to keep his head above water. In the meantime, Paul applied for Covid-19 small-business assistance and continued his yoga practice privately.

It was important to Paul to keep reminding himself that, just like in yoga, every financial life experiences highs and lows, good times and bad, and one must simply be patient, do what needs to be done, and keep an eye on the larger goal. He had thought his goal—that of teaching yoga—was already achieved and he was just living out his lifelong dream, but 2020 made him realize he had an even greater goal than that. After all, Paul's spiritual discipline couldn't thrive unless it was tested. Life had to throw him lefts and rights in addition to ups and downs. Only then would he learn the deeper meanings of yin and yang.

Having everything he valued taken away from him turned out to be the best test of all. Paul endeavored to learn whether he could still thrive while living a non-spiritual lifestyle and saw the experience as a spiritual test, not a financial failure. As such, his management of money paired with his management of his **relationship** to a higher power. 2020 left Paul with hindsight that allowed him to see light in the dark more clearly. What a blessing.

$tuff

The value of practically every object in the world can be assessed with some type of money, the unit that measures **stuff**. Yet the value of each currency, every day, is subject to our human perception of what has value under a given set of circumstances. So, while **stuff** is the most commonly accepted currency, it is, in many ways, the most volatile.

Summing Up Part 1: Purpose

Your life may be nothing like these particular examples, but like each of them, your life is unique and your relationship with the four currencies equally so. Examining your reaction to each of these stories can help you get in touch with what your own values are and give new perspective on how you manage the relevant currencies in your own life, because ultimately, when we talk about money, we're talking about problem solving.

When we talk about money, we also talk about safety and security and your ability to share that security with others. When we talk about money, we talk about all the currencies and how they interact with one another. These currencies are the things we trade to build our lives. By "build" I don't mean building your dream home (although that, too) I mean building your holistic life—your meaningful relationships, your sense of time well spent, your mental and physical health, and your collection of the stuff you need to make all of it happen. When we talk about money, we talk about rising above the mundane; we talk about creating the balanced lives we envision; we talk about caring for all aspects of ourselves and others. Therefore, when we talk about money, we talk about love.

PART 2

The Self

How can you hide from
what never goes away?

HERACLITUS

The Seven Financial Natures

WHEN MY DAUGHTER Sydney was born, I noticed she was a go-with-the-flow kind of kid. When it was time to go to sleep, Sydney lay in bed, often just holding my hand, until sleep arrived in its own good time. When she first learned to ride a bike, she followed the wobbles and rode around in a serpentine manner. Hers was more of an effort to prevent the bike from falling over rather than to make it stay upright. But when my second daughter Kira was born, she was different. Kira was all about imposing her will on the world. When it was time for Kira to go to sleep, she would go if she was ready to rest but not if sleeping might require a lot of effort. For her, learning to ride a bike was a white-knuckle travail until she could make the machine obey her will and go in a perfectly straight line. Because they were both girls, my wife and I knew this wasn't a male/female difference but simply a matter of the two children being born with different natures. Loving and supporting them both in becoming their own best version of the unique people they already were helped us see a truth that now underlies the principles in this book.

When a child is born, it's incredible, a miracle, a life-changing experience for any parent, but then there is a second phase of miraculous amazement:

when you start to notice that child's in-built personality or immutable tendencies. It's impossible to really know where the child's nature comes from except to say "it's in the genes." For me, this realization was life altering. In fact, raising children might be the thing that has helped me most in developing my technique as a financial planner. It helped me conclude that adults, just like children, are only teachable to a certain degree. We are all limited in how much we can change our pre-determined approach to the currencies in our lives. But this isn't a bad thing.

In my youth, I played a lot of sports and coached them, as well. What I learned both from receiving great coaching and coaching others was that it is always more productive to focus on making the most of your strengths than to try to master your weakest skills. Weaknesses are important in that they must not be ignored. Players need to be aware of them. But every coach knows that as part of a team, players must each be utilized to their strengths. Trying to turn someone with an uneven skill set into a mediocre player of all positions would do nothing for a team, as most great teams are collections of specialized players.

In life, if you're married or in any other partnership, this same philosophy applies. But what if the partners' skill sets don't complement one another? And what if you're single and managing finances on your own? While I developed my philosophy as a financial planner, I had to ask myself: In the world of finance, can individuals focus primarily on their strengths, like team players?

To solve this riddle, when I had clients that saved as if prepping for an apocalypse or who were rampant shop-a-holics, I examined those extreme personalities. Instead of telling such people to change their habits, I taught myself to work with, not against, whatever the client's tendencies were, believing the presence of certain weaknesses implied strengths in opposing areas. In the long run, I developed a customizable system to help people of all different personality types achieve effective, long-lasting financial success. The key, in my opinion, is still to focus on strengths but with an emphasis on maximizing both self awareness and peoples' natural motivation to strive for something better.

The Number Seven

Let's talk about the first aspect of that riddle: How can individuals find their financial planning strengths? It all comes down to the number seven.

Seven comes up frequently in cultures all over the world. For instance, there are seven days of the week, seven colors of the rainbow, seven planets revolving around the sun, and seven musical notes in both western and Indian musical systems. The planet Earth has seven continents. In biology, a skin cell regenerates in seven days, and the cells in our bodies are replaced every seven years. Yogic philosophy talks about the body having seven chakras. There are seven stages of grief. Most mammals have seven orifices. The periodic table of elements has seven rows. Seven represents ph neutrality between acids and bases. There are seven celestial bodies visible to the naked eye and seven stars in the Big Dipper. In addition, the number seven figures prominently in Christianity, Judaism, Islam, and Hinduism, which is something I'd love to write an entirely different book about, but for now, let's stick to financial planning.

I have found that there are also seven primary types of people when it comes to how we handle money. These types include people who love to save and those who love to spend, but there are other types, too: Some folks love to invest their money in big schemes. Others thrive by giving it away. Some people are impulsive with money, while others get "analysis paralysis" from considering their choices from every angle. We've all known people who take pride in working hard for their money as well as those always on the lookout for easy money. Having analyzed thousands, perhaps tens of thousands, of individual financial behaviors, I have come up with seven categories that represent all the ways people deal with currency. I call these the seven Financial Natures.

Everyone has a bias toward one of these but is also capable of taking on characteristics of other Natures. Think of your Financial Nature as the most used and well-worn neural pathway you have. You are simply more comfortable with, and used to doing things, a certain way, especially when it comes to spending, saving, and earning currency. That preferred way is your Financial Nature.

These Natures are each complex in their own right and include more than just a person's tendencies around spending and saving. They take into account the emotions people feel around money. For instance, some folks get a thrill when they see big numbers in their savings accounts while others only get that thrill from impulse shopping. Some people feel joy at the sight of a balanced account book while others get that spark from taking risks. Money makes some people feel passionate and others panicky. The seven Financial Natures address these emotional aspects of money as well as the superficial behaviors that go along with them.

The system I'm going to teach you in this book has several puzzle pieces that fit together like cogs in a machine, or, if you prefer, like the seven chakras that enable individuals to attain enlightenment. The set of seven Financial Natures is only the first piece of this system.

The first thing you'll want to do in order make the most of the financial planning system you'll learn here is to go ahead and take the assessment:

ON THE INTERNET, GO TO CURRENCYCAMP.COM OR THIS LINK:

The assessment will simply ask you seven questions and then reveal for you your Financial Nature, at which point, you'll discover that you fall into one of the following categories. Below are very brief descriptions of what are actually much more complex personality types. In-depth descriptions of these types will follow.

1. *Spender*

- ➤ Strengths: energetic, confident, dramatic
- ➤ Weaknesses: mood swings, depression, mania
- ➤ Happiness feels: fun
- ➤ Happiest when: at play

2. *Earner*

- ➤ Strengths: efficient, hard working, disciplined
- ➤ Weaknesses: burnt-out, rigid, over-burdened
- ➤ Happiness feels: satisfying
- ➤ Happiest when: achieving a job well done

3. *Saver*

- ➤ Strengths: prepared, frugal, reserved
- ➤ Weaknesses: cheap, isolated
- ➤ Happiness feels: relaxing
- ➤ Happiest when: safe and comfortable

4. *Investor*

- ➤ Strengths: productive, creative, active
- ➤ Weaknesses: speculative, erratic, addictive
- ➤ Happiness feels: joyful
- ➤ Happiest when: building, creating, making

5. *Lever*

- ➤ Strengths: collaboration, problem solving
- ➤ Weaknesses: opportunistic, lazy, manipulative
- ➤ Happiness feels: easy, efficient
- ➤ Happiest when: beating the system (by creating a better one)

6. *Giver*

- ➤ Strengths: intuition, leadership, vision
- ➤ Weaknesses: isolation, martyrdom
- ➤ Happiness feels: spiritually enlightened
- ➤ Happiest when: giving to others

7. *Taker*

- ➤ Strengths: reactive, instinctive, resourceful
- ➤ Weaknesses: impulsive, chaotic, panicky
- ➤ Happiness feels: exciting
- ➤ Happiest when: taking risks

There is no hierarchy among these types, but I have arranged them in a specific order because it's the order that matters. This is demonstrated in the diagram below:

FIGURE I

We're all Monkeys with Money

A 2005 study at Yale experimented with teaching capuchin monkeys how to use money. Scientists presented the monkeys with wooden tokens and taught them that these could be exchanged for food. Not only that, but there was one exchange mechanism that gave the monkeys one grape per token, predictably, while another one operated more like a slot machine. Sometimes inserting a token would yield nothing, but other times it yielded a wealth of grapes. Then, the monkeys had opportunities to exchange their tokens with whichever mechanism and at whatever frequency they wished.

Researchers found that some monkeys hoarded their tokens, while others loved to gamble. Some used their tokens responsibly, according to the need for sustenance, while others saved up and binged later. In other words, the monkey population displayed the same distribution of behaviors that humans do, across the board. Monkeys, like humans, have unique personalities, and that applies to their financial as well as emotional and psychological lives.

For me, learning about this study reinforced my understanding of the fact that every population has a natural distribution of individuals who assess value differently. Any group of men tested like the monkeys will show the same distribution of behaviors. Any group of women will also show the same distribution. Our natural, individual relationship with currency is not based upon gender, culture, race, or any predictable factor. It is simply true that any cross-section of a population contains—and, for balance, must contain—the full complement of seven Financial Natures.

These Natures can be thwarted due to cultural factors. For instance, a culture that only values conservative saving may deride impulsive, emotional thrill-seekers, gamblers, and risky investors. The pervasiveness of this attitude represses the natural (and very important) skill sets of the Takers, Spenders, Investors, and Givers of the world. When these types are made to feel as if their instincts are wrong, it robs them of the ability to hone the best aspects of their unique skill sets. Because people cannot change their essential Financial Natures, such a situation simply brings out the worst in them. Denying their intuitions and feelings may cause them to fail to access an entire realm of essential knowledge.

By the same token, a culture that values freedom, intuition, risk-taking, and adventure may shun the more conservative Earners and Savers that inevitably exist in any society, to the detriment of both the larger group and each individual. Without support, such people will simply descend into maladaptive manifestations of their Natures such as hoarding, isolating, and rigid thought patterns.

Turning the Knob

Once people accept that these different Financial Natures inevitably exist, and once they discover which category they have been assigned from birth, the trick is to learn how to create the ideal state of flow for your particular Nature. Teaching how to do that is, in fact, the purpose of this book. Key to that flow is an understanding of the dangerous extremes to which each Financial Nature can lean. It's crucial to learn to catch oneself before such behaviors get out of control.

The way we do this (and I apologize for speaking a bit abstractly right now, but I'll get into practical details as we move forward) is to learn to scan our beings like pilots scan airplane safety features during flight checks. You could also view it as being like the way yogis scan their bodies (how do my toes feel? Ankles? Knees? Hips? Breath?) during yoga practice. Once you learn to evaluate how you're spending, earning, saving, investing, borrowing, leveraging, donating, and receiving, it becomes quite easy to tweak your behavior in order to stay in the correct balance for your Financial Nature.

When you learn to do your own personal financial scan, you'll find disorder and disease early on, before it ruins your plans. After all, you can allocate the currency of time, can't you? If you carefully go over your weekly planner and discover you have double-booked yourself so that you are expected to be in two places at once, you can make a phone call, reschedule one of your commitments, and solve the problem. The same thing applies to your financial life. It's simply a matter of learning how to scan your financial life as easily as businesspeople scan their appointment books, yogis scan their bodies, and pilots scan their airplane safety features. When this skill becomes a habit, you can do it almost without thinking, allowing you to fix little problems before they become big ones.

I think of the little problems you find in these scans as blocks to what would otherwise be a natural flow—like the way the flow of electricity can be blocked by the flipping of a switch. The following diagram illustrates how I view these blockages. Do you see how one of these dials can be turned the wrong way and stop the flow? If you know how to scan for what's wrong in your financial life, all you have to do is identify the blockage, turn the dial, and get that flow going again.

FIGURE 2

Now that you understand where we're going, philosophically, we can get into the nitty-gritty of learning each Financial Nature and the practical application of the system in this book. It all hinges on acceptance of the fact that seven Financial Natures exist and that each is necessary in our world.

Each Nature must be nurtured to its best manifestation so that we can all learn to find and eliminate financial blockages as easily as we scan our homes, cars, and sidewalks for potential hazards—something we do instinctively, on the fly. Below, you'll find in-depth descriptions of each Financial Nature, but first, I'm going to teach you about some details that will help you fully comprehend the range of skills and abilities in each Nature. These details are called Distortion Fields and Motivations.

Distortion Fields and Motivations

THE FINANCIAL PLANNING system I have developed—based upon the Financial Natures described above—is designed to help everyone, from those who constantly endeavor to be responsible with their finances all the way to people who prefer to live by the seat of their pants and never think about money. In order to show you how one system can help all types of people, we're going to start with an extreme example, that of a fictional character I'll call Freddie FreeSpirit.

Much learning does not teach understanding

HERACLITUS

Freddie FreeSpirit is an example of the financial nature called Taker, whose primary way of being is to react impulsively. The Taker is one who captures life and drinks it in, like taking a photograph you can keep forever. With this Financial Nature, Freddie takes his time, takes pleasure in every moment, and takes it easy. Takers tend to intellectualize life less and excel at things that require great instincts like music, art, and athletics.

Freddie's nature is to never plan or manage any of the currencies in his life. His **money, time, relationships,** and **health** are all things he deals with on the spur of the moment. Freddie is the ultimate devil-may-care type of person. Others often roll their eyes at his irresponsible-seeming nature, but, let's face it, people also secretly envy him. They wonder how he manages to survive year after year with so little stress and so little planning … and so much fun!

As the ultimate embodiment of the Taker (an emotionally reactive personality) our Freddie is a surfer who lives with roommates in a bungalow near the beach, works at a surf shop, and hangs out the rest of the time. Bonfires on the beach are his greatest pleasure and where he meets new friends. Freddie has always been lucky with the ladies, too, and they seem to intuitively know that good old Freddie will never be tied down.

But Freddy has goals, too. He'd like to become a pro surfer and travel to the great surf spots on the globe. So, what's holding him back? Just like most of us, Freddie takes action toward his goal but always seems to fall short. Traveling the world costs money, and try as he might, he can't seem to save enough for a bus ticket to the next town over, much less a flight to the Great Barrier Reef. Let's see if we can help frustrated Freddie identify the blocks to maximizing his free-spirited potential.

Distortion Fields

If we take another, closer look at the wheel of Financial Natures, we can see that Taker lies between Giver and Spender. Each individual tends to exist in his or her Nature as if it is the eye of a hurricane. The Taker, for instance, will swirl around in a whirlwind that touches on its neighboring Natures. Some compare this circular motion to a hamster on an exercise wheel—always running but never getting anywhere.

Takers are *reactors*, so they tend to be instinctual, impulsive, and exciting but can also tend toward becoming Givers—visionary types who are natural leaders that love helping others. On the other side, they can act like Spenders—confident, feelings-based personalities that love to play. See figure 3, below.

At his worst, Freddie FreeSpirit will manifest the leadership qualities of the Giver but lack the type of ability that enables one to make a plan of action. At his best, he will gain the natural confidence and action-orientation of the Spender. In short, it's good for Freddie to move in one direction on the wheel: clockwise. It will do him no good to move in the other direction. There is a way for Freddie to successfully embody the traits of the Giver if he wants to, but it will take a few chapters to get there, so stick with me.

Freddie's tendency, like all of ours, is to try to travel forward from the eye of his hurricane. Just as he is about to enter and take on the deeply feeling nature of the Spender (a nature that could help him leverage his naturally emotional way of being into something more confident) he somehow fails to achieve that. He gets caught up in the swirling winds that convey him around the eye of the hurricane (his true Taker Nature) to the other side, where he confronts his Giver Nature.

The problem with a Taker trying to take on the Nature of a Giver is that unless he has prepared extensively, he isn't ready to succeed here. So, rather than becoming a successful Giver, Freddie will be picked up again by the hurricane winds that take him around again toward his tendency to act like a Spender. And the cycle continues ad infinitum like the hamster on the wheel, so that Freddie is constantly striving but never getting anywhere. But if Freddie knows the technique for how to successfully embody the next Nature in the wheel, he will finally learn to break his old habits and make progress.

So, to summarize, the seven Financial Natures exist in a certain order for a reason. In order to move forward in life and achieve goals, a person must know his Nature, then learn the tricks of embodying the dominant energy

FIGURE 3

of the next Financial Nature, always progressing in clockwise order around the wheel. Soon, I'll teach Freddie, and you, how to do this. But first, I have to show you an important detail about the Financial Natures. I call it The Three Motivations.

The Three Motivations

Knowing that Freddie FreeSpirit is a Taker tells us he has the strengths of being resourceful and action-oriented because he reacts on impulse, much like an animal. Without having to think, and often without being able to verbalize why, he senses the right way to go and which action to take—this is exactly what makes him such a great surfer. Without people like Freddie, our world would lack athletes, artists, and other quick thinkers with access to their instinctive, animal natures. But there is still something we don't know about Freddie. What motivates him?

Why does Freddie want to become a pro surfer? That *why* is incredibly important if we want to help him. In my experience, people are primarily motivated by one of three things: the desire to Protect, the desire to Manage, and the desire to Pursue.

PROTECT

Those who want to Protect are deeply informed by the past and tend to be motivated by a desire to preserve what they have or even preserve a legacy. Protectors are reliable and consistent, but their tendency to live in the past causes them to avoid opportunities for growth and innovation.

If Freddy is a Protector, his desire to become a pro-surfer may be based in the fact that his father was a pro-surfer and he is determined to carry on the family legacy. Or perhaps Freddie is a lot more aware of the passage of **time** than he lets on, and he wants to secure his reputation for all time before he gets too old to surf.

PURSUE

Pursuers are the opposite of Protectors. These people are motivated by their visions of a bright future. They always go after what's next, take on passions and interests with enthusiasm, but often fail to stop and figure out all the details. Sometimes Pursuers will abandon one passionate interest before it has reached fruition in favor of the next idea that comes along, so their action-oriented, future-thinking nature can backfire. Pursuers are often big-picture thinkers who benefit from being able to delegate the tasks of their projects because they lack the patience and perfectionism required to complete each one in a methodical, step-by-step manner.

If Freddie is motivated by a desire to Pursue, that means the naturally instinctive, spontaneous manner he has as a Taker is taken to the utmost extreme. In this case, he wants to become a pro-surfer in order to ride waves that have never been ridden before. He doesn't care about leaving a legacy so much as he wants to fulfill all his big-wave surfing dreams as soon as possible and then move on to something bigger. The urge to dream big, make those dreams come true, and always live in the moment—this would motivate Freddie if he were a Taker that was motivated to Pursue.

MANAGE

Managers are those at a third point somewhat between the extremes of Protector and Pursuer. These are the thinkers, the planners, the perfectionists. Managers cross their T's and dot their I's. They go over the details of their documents, plans, and projects with the intention of doing things right the first time. They're not as easy-going and devil-may-care as the Pursuers, but they're not as conservative and careful as the Protectors. Managers get things done but can be hampered by their perfectionistic tendencies.

If you know someone who asks a lot of questions before giving input on a topic or who rethinks the logic behind every decision, this is a Manager. By contrast, Pursuers are typically too busy "thinking big" to worry about details, while Protectors are typically too concerned about doing things "the old-fashioned way" to consider innovative ideas.

If Freddy is motivated by a desire to Manage, then his pro-surfer ambition is based upon an understanding of the step-by-step process of becoming a pro-surfer, analysis of the benefits attached to it, and an awareness that his surfing resume shows him, realistically, to be a contender.

The Protector is like a pirate protecting his gold. The Pursuer is like

PROTECT

Preserves the status quo
Rejects innovation

MANAGE

Focuses on the present
Seeks perfection

PURSUE

Innovates the future
*Lacks attention
to detail*

FIGURE 4

a long-distance runner trying to cover as much ground as possible. The Manager is like a construction foreman who gathers all the tools, materials, and personnel to build a house and won't be distracted until the job is done.

Now that you understand there are seven Financial Natures, three different categories of Motivation, and a tendency for each Nature to be the eye of a hurricane that touches on its neighboring Natures, this more-detailed diagram will make sense to you:

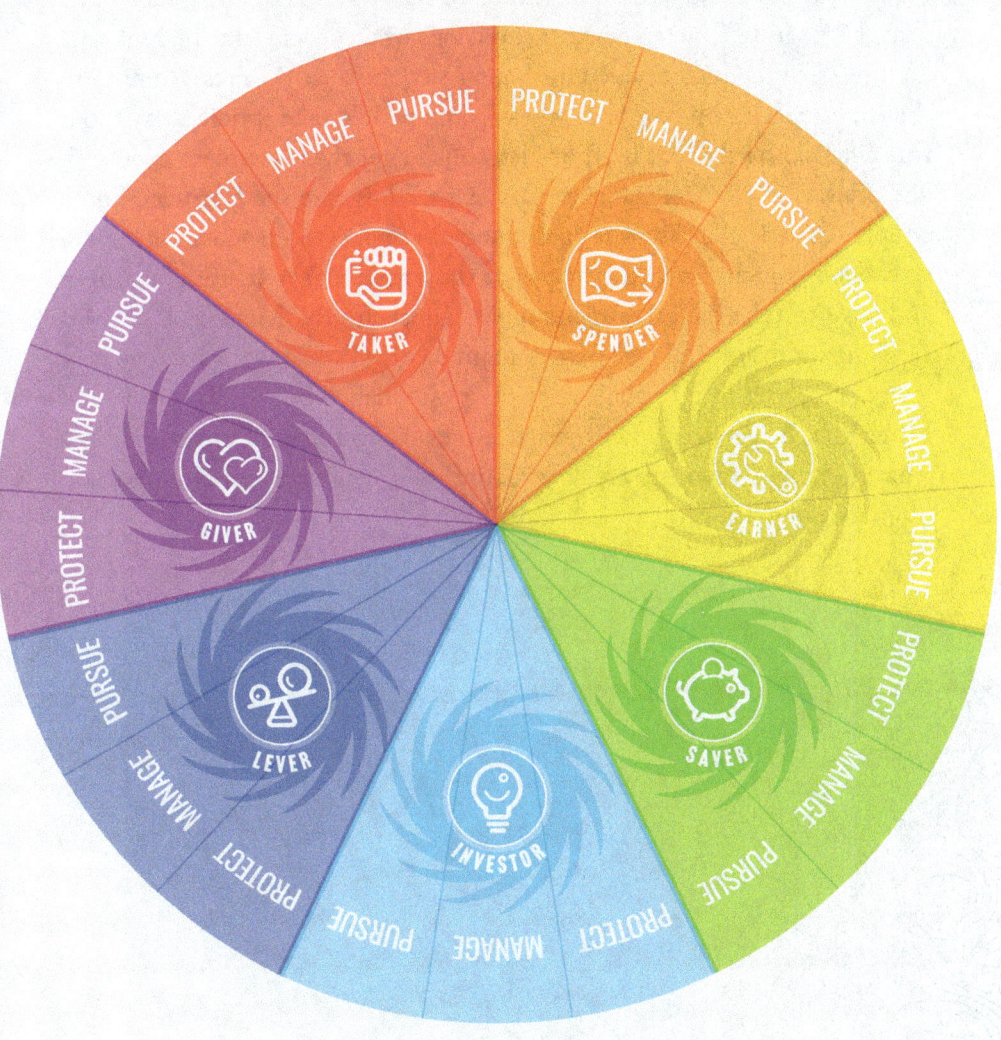

FIGURE 5

What's Your Motivation?

It's easy to figure out which of the three Motivations dominate anyone's Financial Nature. The truth becomes obvious when people take the Financial Nature assessment mentioned in chapter two, because they tend to react to the experience in one of three ways. Some people take it quickly without thinking too hard about it. They just want to get the assessment over with and often skip some of the necessary steps. Those are the Pursuers. Some people think so hard about each question and second-guess their own answers so much that when they get the answer, they doubt it's correct and have to take the assessment again. Those are the Managers. A third type may refuse to take the assessment at all. They don't want any new information that might contradict their established beliefs. Those are the Protectors. It has been my experience that Protectors and Pursuers know what they are. Managers aren't sure, but their language and questions are often a dead giveaway.

The Seven Natures in Detail

O NE DAY, ABOUT 15 years ago, I found myself at a blackboard. A question had come up in my mind that seemed worthy of exploring. Essentially, it went something like this: If we use our resources and money to try to improve our **relationships** with ourselves and others, then how do our **relationships** with money help make that happen? I picked up the chalk and graphed a visual representation of the **relationships** people have with money. The exercise produced seven distinct **relationships**.

Like musical notes, these **relationships** repeat to form financial octaves. People tend to prefer one of these notes. Like musical notes (doh, re, mi, fa, so, la, ti), or colors of the rainbow, these relationships repeat to form financial octaves. People tend to resonate or prefer a certain color or sound. My daughters favorite color is green and Homer Simpson resonates with "doh!" My financial preference is leverage. It's a natural bias that has led to funny moments when played out of tune. Each of us prefers a certain type of **relationship** with our currency, and we use words to express that **relationship**. It took years for these word pairings to fully flesh out in my mind, but I present them to you here so that you can enjoy seeing if you resonate with the words that match your Financial Nature. You have permission to have fun with what follows. Enjoy, relax, go easy on yourself —it's all good.

The unlike is joined together,
and from differences results
the most beautiful harmony

HERACLITUS

The Spender

- ➤ *Strengths: energetic, confident, dramatic*

- ➤ *Pitfalls: mood swings, depression, mania*

- ➤ *Happiness feels: fun*

- ➤ *Happiest when: at play*

SPENDERS SPECIALIZE IN the Financial State called *feel*. (I will explain more about Financial States in chapter seven.) They are hyper-aware of their feelings and consciously make decisions based upon them. The most obvious financial connection between Spenders and their feelings is a tendency to use shopping as a balm for their nerves. Some call it "retail therapy." On the plus side, at their best, Spenders tend to be excellent shoppers—always finding bargains, providing for the family's needs, and purchasing items that truly make them feel fulfilled.

It's important to note that Spenders act from an external motivation to meet the needs of the world. Later, you will see very similar behavior when we discuss the nature of the Giver, but with the Giver, spending comes from a place of internal motivation—a place of passion rather than empathy. These emotional differences are important to understand, because the Financial Natures are more than just the ways certain people act, they are also tied to the mindsets that determine why people do the things they do.

Spenders aren't afraid to spend! If Spenders have a problem, they'll throw money at it … sometimes too much money. This is where the downside of this Nature comes in. Spenders tend to live at a Level of Sufficiency, meaning that their income fluctuates up and down. (I will explain more about Financial Levels in chapter six.) Whenever they have enough money, they go out and spend it all until their bank account is in the red. When they get paid again, the cycle repeats itself.

Spenders are action-oriented, and their active lifestyles are fueled by emotion. They have a great deal of emotional awareness, which some call emotional intelligence. So, while Spenders might go out and shop away their feelings, they typically know whether they're upset or just having fun. In the best case scenario, such shopping trips might lead Spenders to appointments with their therapists. There, Spenders can spend some time working out ways to solve emotional problems without emptying their wallets.

SPENDER MOTIVATIONS

Empathize

SPENDERS WITH A MOTIVATION TO PROTECT

Spender/Protectors are emotionally aware people who use their empathic and fun-loving personalities to keep the world safe. They make great teachers, parents, coaches, and counselors. Their love of spending for the sake of fun can also make them great event organizers, corporate buyers, and decorators. Keeping their spending habits under control tends to be a challenge for Spenders, generally, but Spender/Protectors are beloved for how their empathetic Natures inspire them to build solid foundations by spending quality **time** with loved ones as well as spending their energy on exciting activities.

Neutralize

SPENDERS WITH A MOTIVATION TO MANAGE

Spenders who Manage examine their feelings in detail. This can lead to positive results such as the ability to have deeply honest **relationships**.

Those who examine their feelings can help partners who block out their feelings to get in touch with what's really going on, deep down. On the other hand, Spender/Managers can also go down the road to obsession and hypochondria. So, it's important for Spender/Managers to learn to neutralize the tendency to overthink their feelings.

Spenders will benefit by having the flexibility to move into the *think* Financial State in order to cycle through the States (more on the Financial States in chapter seven), but that means learning the new skill of *thinking* instead of *feeling*, rather than thinking too much about feelings.

Strategize

SPENDERS WITH A MOTIVATION TO PURSUE

Due to their highly emotional nature and desire to always see what's around the next corner, Spender/Pursuers can be incredibly fun companions who stop at nothing in the pursuit of a good time. However, their tendency to overspend will likely come back to haunt them. Spender/Pursuers will benefit by consciously strategizing in order to differentiate wants from needs. The key is to identify the urge to spend as it comes up and then prioritize such urges by asking, "Which of these items really needs to be bought, versus which ones are just for fun?" With knowledge of the available budget, a Spender/Pursuer can stay within bounds, but it will take strategy and discipline.

PITFALLS FOR SPENDERS

Because Spenders may be subject to mood swings, they can become emotionally paralyzed when down or depressed. By contrast, they can become irrational when happy or manic. The danger for Spenders is in getting stuck in either of these extremes. It's natural for Spenders to swing from one mood to another, and trying to stop them from doing so will only end in frustration. The key to getting the best from Spenders is to keep them always swinging, always moving through their feelings, never stagnating in one set feeling for too long, and avoiding the extremes of mood that can drag them into stagnation. As long as their world is dramatic and fun, the feelings will flow, the currencies will get spent, and Spenders will be at their best. Viewing emotional swings as going from left to right instead of up and down can help reframe this pitfall in a more positive light.

Distortion Field

Spenders live in the eye of a hurricane whose edges touch the Earner Nature on one side and the Taker Nature on the other. Spenders will benefit from learning to embody the thoughtful state that characterizes the Earner, while trying to stay away from the temptation to react to thoughts like a Taker.

A Spender who reacts impulsively is dangerous indeed to his own wallet, but a Spender who thinks carefully like an Earner, while also staying in touch with his feelings, can spend in ways that are truly beneficial. In this case, the Spender's action-oriented lifestyle and tendency to "put his money where his mouth is" is useful, especially to more cautious friends and family members who need a Spender in their lives to take action and make things happen.

Spender CHARACTERISTICS CHART

Superpowers	*High energy, confident, empathic, sensitive, fun, dramatic, exciting, results-oriented*
Weaknesses	*Extreme mood swings, paralyzing depression, stagnation, overly dramatic, envious, a spendthrift, doesn't think things through*
Keywords	*Emotion, energy, drama, sensitive, sentimental, feeling, fun, confident, excitement buying, spending, finding*
Paired With	*Feel Financial State, Sufficient Financial Level, second chakra (These pairings are explained in chapters 6 and 7)*
Left Distortion Field	*Leaning toward the Taker Nature, Spenders tend to rely on animalistic instincts instead of an awareness of their feelings.*
Right Distortion Field	*Trending toward the Earner Nature, Spenders will become more determined and goal-oriented, gaining the ability to allocate resources wisely—all while staying in touch with their feelings.*

SPENDERS YOU'VE HEARD OF

The Spender as a Superhero

In popular culture, there are many superheroes whose special powers are derived from accidental events such as being bit by an insect or being exposed to radiation. One of these famous superheroes has the agility of a spider and can spin webs to swing from place to place in a jiffy. I liken this character to a Spender because of all that swinging. Emotional mood swings characterize the Spender, although, like with this superhero, those mood swings can also be used for good. When Spenders are motivated, they get out there and spend **time,** spend **money,** and spend energy solving problems and helping to save the world. That's the active, empathetic nature of a Spender.

Spenders in History

History is full of Spender-types who channeled their feelings into their art. Some of these include the famous painter Vincent Van Gogh, the legendary comedian Robin Williams, and the musician Kurt Kobain. Other famous artists who have admitted to manic depression or other extreme feelings include modern actors Jim Carrey and Kristen Bell as well as historical painters Frida Kahlo and Edvard Munch. In fact, Munch's famous painting "The Scream" is a pretty literal depiction of a panic attack.

Writers inhabit this world, too, and those believed to have had schizophrenia, depression, or bi-polar disorder include David Foster Wallace, Jack Kerouac, Theodore Roethke, Edgar Allen Poe, Tennessee Williams, Ernest Hemingway, Virginia Woolf, Emily Dickinson, Anne Sexton, Sylvia Plath, Dylan Thomas, and many more. Famous musicians who have battled depression include Brian Wilson of The Beach Boys, Syd Barrett of Pink Floyd, Ray Davies of the Kinks, and Sinead O'Connor. Overall, it is simply well known that great artists of all kinds often enjoy (and yet also struggle with) lives and careers driven by strong feelings.

It is of note that many famous artists achieved success by channeling their feelings into at least one art form, but they couldn't have become famous without an audience. We enjoy the work of these famous Spender types because of their unique abilities to express that which we all feel, to some degree or another.

Another characteristic of many of the above-named artists is that not only were they unique in their artistic expression, but many were iconoclasts in their lifestyles as well. Bold and unafraid of breaking social conventions, such strong-willed individuals are responsible for wide-ranging changes in society and the liberation of social norms to allow for expanded avenues of personal expression. Entire subcultures have developed around some of these expressive individuals—all because those with an advanced ability to express feelings give the rest of us the opportunity to jump for joy, cry, or scream, which we might otherwise have bottled up.

Spenders In the Bible

The apostle Paul is a good example of a Spender Nature in the Bible. When it comes to mood swings, he's your man. In the beginning, he was a hater of Christ who was highly motivated to destroy him. During this time he was called Saul. A murderous zealot, Saul put many believers in prison and even delivered death warrants against them, spending **money, time,** and all his resources to relentlessly pursue his agenda. Later, he was struck blind when Christ confronted him, asking, "Why are you persecuting me?"

At this point, Saul had a revelation and saw himself and his actions in a new light. As a result, he changed into Paul: a humble, loving, kind, and even sacrificial promoter of Christ. During both phases of his life, one can see Paul's intense devotion to his cause and willingness to spend all his resources in pursuit of it. Yet, the mood swings that can make a Spender inconsistent are also present with Paul.

SPENDERS I'VE KNOWN

Mary

Mary (a Spender) came to me for help with a very specific problem: She spent too much money on shoes. She simply couldn't get enough of shoes. Spending money this way had, she felt, become a type of mania and she wanted my help to stop. I analyzed all her finances and came to the conclusion that she made a very good living, and it was easy to ensure that the appropriate amount went into savings, bill paying, and long-term investments. At the end of the day, I told her she had a certain budget for fun money, and her shoe budget was part of it. She hung her head in shame. I said, "Chin up!"

"If buying shoes is what you like to do, then why stop?" I asked, adding, "I also wonder: are these shoes investments? If you keep them in the box, can they be resold?" Whether or not they were useful as investments, I told her, "It's your fun money and you can do whatever you want with it. But if you want to do something else, then you could cut back on the shoes. It's a choice only you can make."

Knowing the nature of a Spender, I was aware that spending brought her joy in life, so the last thing I'd want to do is take that away. All I needed to do with Mary was let her know she had a right to pursue fun whatever way she wanted, within this part of her budget.

Mary was a Spender, but her Motivational style was Manager. Although her Spender Nature had led her into this wild shoe-buying habit, deep down, she didn't want to live with the impulsiveness of a Pursuer or the conservatism of a Protector. She wanted to do what was logical, based upon the math. Now that she understood she wasn't being judged for her shoe habit (and stopped judging herself), she could look at the dollar amount she spent on shoes monthly and assess the value of that expenditure in terms of what else it could buy.

In the end, Mary realized that because her job offered her discounts on shoes and apparel, she had gone a little crazy with the temptation such discounts and sales provided. What she really wanted to do, though, was go on a vacation to a spa, so she re-allocated her shoe budget to achieve that. Now that she had a clearer sense of the dollars and cents involved, Mary was able to lift herself out of the emotionally-charged shoe-buying craze yet still enjoy spending on other types of fun that fit in her budget.

This was a real victory for Mary. She came to me expecting a reprimand for her fiscal irresponsibility but left with nothing but encouragement and a set of choices that put her in the driver's seat. When solving any type of currency problem, it's always important to acknowledge that different people get their enjoyment from life in different ways, and that fact must be respected.

Mrs. Johnson

Mrs. Johnson was a Spender who was very in-touch with the neighboring nature: Earner. In terms of the Distortion Field of the Spender, she was trending in the right direction, meaning toward the *thinking* nature of the Earner rather than back toward the *reacting* nature of the Taker. However, every month she spent her surplus income like the world was ending tomorrow. She wanted to prepare for retirement and allocate her money more wisely but simply didn't know how. She came to me saying she figured the solution had something to do with investing capital but didn't know enough about investing to take on the challenge herself. She also didn't know how to stop her own wild spending habits.

To help her re-assess her spending, I brought the issue back to its core, which was the emotional value of her behavior. I asked her, "How do you feel when you earn a commission check?"

She said, "Great!"

I replied, "And what do you do when you feel that way?"

"I spend it!" she answered.

I challenged her with, "Are you satisfied with that experience?" I knew she wasn't, because that's why she had come to me in the first place.

Dejected, she replied, "No."

I asked what it would take to make her life better.

Mrs. Johnson admitted she wanted to figure out how to save, but this wasn't something that came naturally to her. Her emotional happy place was "fun," but saving and investing didn't feel fun to her. I knew that to get her to willingly save money, I'd have to help her see saving as something that could be fun, so it was helpful when she readily admitted that investing her money would at least yield dividends, so that would be more fun than putting it in savings. I presented her with some options that let her select an investment that would bring her joy, making the decision fun for her, not a chore.

Some clients, like Earners and Savers, would be more motivated by an experience that fed their need for comfort, stability, and relaxation, but knowing Spenders like I do, I understood that the only way Mrs. Johnson would start investing was if I made it fun and easy.

Do you see why knowing the Financial Natures is so crucial to helping yourself and others improve? How one presents information can have a great bearing on how that information is received. The Financial Natures provide guidance in exactly how to do that.

The Earner

- *Strengths: hard working, determined, efficient*

- *Pitfalls: rigidity, aggression, poor life/work balance*

- *Happiness feels: satisfying*

- *Happiest when: at work*

WHEN YOU THINK of folks who are proud of living "by the sweat of their brow," it's highly likely these are Earners. Present in all walks of life, Earners tend to become absorbed in their work and take satisfaction in a job well done. Earners like to move forward quickly and efficiently and measure their success in life by material progress. American culture heaps rewards upon its disciplined, goal-directed, efficient Earners. Earners' daytimers are always chock full of obligations, while their money tends to be pre-allocated before it is even earned. Everything in an Earner's life has a place, and everything is in its place. They resonate at a frenetic frequency and function as if on a cosmic treadmill. Put simply: Earners can't sit still.

The trick to being a successful Earner is to remember that success is more than just money. One must keep an eye on the big picture and balance the time spent on health, relationships, and stuff acquisition. Yet, there's no telling what currency any individual values most, so there are also Earners who strive this intensely for non-monetary currencies. These people may be deeply dedicated to building relationships, athletic prowess, or specific skills rather than their bank accounts, but just like with money-centric Earners, their focus on the currency they value is intense, organized, and indefatigable, tending toward an imbalanced approach to life's many currencies.

EARNER MOTIVATIONS

Generate

EARNERS WITH A MOTIVATION TO PROTECT

Earners who are motivated to Protect can be closed off and solitary. They work incessantly to ensure financial stability, but with no end in sight. That's why they tend to stay at the Financial Level of Efficiency and not above (more on Financial Levels in chapter six). Such Earners would benefit from learning the skill of investing. In chapter six you'll learn more about how when you invest your income in such a way that it provides a trouble-free secondary income (Financial Levels 5-7, Productivity through Inductivity) you can gain the security you crave without sacrificing the currency of **time**. Also, Earner/Protectors would do well to set financial goals and learn not to exceed them. When those goals are met, it's time to stop working and play with your kids or take a vacation.

Allocate

EARNERS WITH A MOTIVATION TO MANAGE

Managers like to allocate their **time** and stay organized. The same is true for Earners, generally, so an Earner/Manager is an allocator extraordinaire. These individuals are incredibly reliable in the sense that they keep an impeccable day timer and are known for being punctual and predictable. Unfortunately, life can't always be planned, so the challenge for Earner/Managers is to detect moments when spontaneity is required and let themselves break away from their set agendas. It might be painful at first, but in the long run, their **relationships** will benefit.

Automate

The forward-moving motivation to Pursue tempers the Earner Nature quite a bit. While other Earners tend to be dedicated to their agendas and calendars with ferocious precision, Earner/Pursuers will be more likely to break out of their proscribed routines in order to seek new opportunities. Although Earners tend to work so hard that they stay at the level of Efficiency and don't tend to make productive investments, Pursuers are the Earners most likely to see the value of investing their savings at Financial Levels five through seven in order to automate an effortless second income. Getting the money flowing in is the point, after all, so if Earner/Pursuers can get that security with less work, why not? Such secondary income opportunities simply free up Earner/Pursuers for finding additional types of work or play that fascinate them anew.

PITFALLS FOR EARNERS

Side effects of the Earner personality include a tendency to ignore non-monetary currencies like **relationships** and **health**. Earners take their responsibilities seriously and often work harder, faster, and longer than others. Often, they feel they are solely responsible for solving problems, and this can lead to them shutting out others whose help might be useful. An Earner can become a work-a-holic, which can be a lonely existence indeed. A partner who once admired the Earner's hardworking nature eventually realizes he or she will never be as important as the Earner's profession. Earners' children often grow up feeling as if they had an absent parent. When it comes to **relationships**, parents need to be there for their kids in more ways than one, and Earners often neglect that emotional piece of the puzzle. They aren't the only Financial Nature to do this, but when Earners do it, their motivation to work hard is often what drives the behavior.

EARNER

DISTORTION FIELDS

Earners exist between the Financial Natures of Spender and Saver, which means when they deviate from their hard-working Natures, they tend to swirl around between the easygoing ways of the Spender and the conservative ways of the Saver—two opposites. Being inclined to thoughtlessly spend one minute and obsessively save the next can result in what psychologists term "cognitive dissonance"—a confusion caused by thinking two opposing things at once.

This problem is caused by the fact that although Earners are hardworking (and typically financially successful) that doesn't mean they always know just how to manage the money they make. They wonder, "Should I use the money for fun? Or should I save it for retirement?" After all, the Earner's specialty is earning currency, not managing the different ways to spend or save it.

As with all Financial Natures, being aware of the pitfalls of your Nature helps you get one step ahead of the problem, so Earners would benefit from having a financial planner, accountant, or simply a wise spouse to allocate the funds appropriately. Having the right partner in life is helpful for every Nature, but none more-so than the Earner, who often needs reminders that life is for living, not just working.

Earner CHARACTERISTICS CHART

Superpowers	*Hard working, industrious, determined, efficient, competent, reliable, good time management skills, boldness in action*
Weaknesses	*Tendency toward burnout, rigidity, and being over-analytical. Can be overly aggressive and have a poor work/life balance. Obsessive. Tends to get stuck in "the rat race."*
Keywords	*Work, satisfaction, thought, effort, bold, industrious, determined, dynamic, busy, sharp, intense, direct, allocate, analyze, efficient*
Paired With	*Think Financial State, Efficient Financial Level, third chakra (These pairing are explained in chapters 6 and 7)*
Left Distortion Field	*Trending left toward Spender, Earners adopt that Nature's high energy, fun-loving, empathetic ways but tend to be less responsible with their money.*
Right Distortion Field	*Trending right toward Saver, Earners become extremely frugal and confident that they are always prepared, which makes them feel relaxed and in control.*

EARNERS YOU'VE HEARD OF

The Earner as a Superhero

All superheroes that embody the trait of super speed are great comparisons for the hardworking Earner Nature. Clad in psychological spandex, Earners zip from one project to another, saving the day here, there, and everywhere. If you need someone to take care of business, the Earners in your life will be at the ready … as long as you don't thwart their carefully made plans.

Some might think speed-based superheroes are spontaneous and always on call, but this speedster sets an agenda for both **time** and **stuff** and rushes from one set task to another all day long, barely allocating exactly the right amount of **time** in-between tasks for transportation and transitions. To get the best out of flash-fast Earners, provide them with meals, health drinks, caffeine, headache tablets, and whatever else they need so they can keep going going going. One thing is for sure, they never want to stop earning the currency of most value to them.

Earners in History

MICHAEL JORDAN

Michael Jordan's long-time coach Phil Jackson has written that while Jordan had great athletic gifts, it was his hard work that made him a legend in the game of basketball. For instance, when he first entered the NBA, Jordan's jump shot wasn't good enough, so he spent his off-season taking hundreds of shots a day until he perfected this crucial skill.

Famously cut from his varsity basketball team in high school, Jordan developed a deeply humble attitude and knew that hard work would be the secret to his success. Said Jordan:

> *"My attitude is if you push me towards something that you think is a weakness, then I will turn that perceived weakness into a strength."*

As such, he practiced his ball handling, quickness, and shooting for hours every day until he was reinstated to the varsity team and never took his position as a player for granted again. His hard work wasn't just in the realm of the physical, either. He also shot for success in other ways, including creative visualization. Jordan has written:

> *"I visualized where I wanted to be, what kind of player I wanted to become. I knew exactly where I wanted to go, and I focused on getting there."*

Believed by many to be the greatest basketball player of all time, by the end of his career, Jordan's accomplishments included six NBA Finals Most Valuable Player Awards, ten scoring titles (both all-time records), five MVP awards, ten all-NBA First Team designations, nine All-Defensive First Team honors, fourteen NBA All-Star Game selections, three All-Star Game MVP Awards, three steals titles, and the 1988 NBA Defensive Player of the Year Award. He holds the NBA record for career regular season scoring average and career playoff scoring average. In 1999 he was named the 20th Century's greatest North American athlete by ESPN and was second only to Babe Ruth on the Associated Press' list of Athletes of the Century. He was twice inducted into the Naismith Memorial Basketball Hall of Fame, became a member of the FIBA Hall of Fame in 2015, and was a member of the 1992 United States Men's Olympic basketball team. Everyone who has ever written about Jordan agrees that his hard-working nature made him a legendary sports figure.

Earners in the Bible

The Bible urges its followers to be hard working but also to take days of rest. It actually admonishes against work-a-holism when it gets in the way of life's more important currencies, such as in Matthew 6:19-21.

> *"Do not lay up for yourselves treasures on Earth, where moth and rust destroy and where thieves break in and steal, but lay up for yourselves treasures in Heaven, where neither moth nor rust destroys*

and where thieves do not break in and steal. For where your treasure is, there your heart will be also.

That said, the Bible is full of hard-working characters, the most prominent of which is Timothy. A soldier, athlete, and farmer, Timothy is known for his self discipline. He is chosen by Paul to help preach the gospel because he is reliable, punctual, and perfectionistic in all he does—the ultimate Earner. 2 Timothy 2:3-6 states:

An athlete is not crowned unless he competes according to the rules. It is the hard-working farmer who ought to have the first share of the crops.

As a soldier, Timothy understands hierarchy, so he becomes a pastor who lives in service to his higher-up, which in this case was God. As such, he earned respect from his boss. As a farmer, he understood that nature works in mysterious ways and never at the whims of man, so that meant getting up early and tending to the fields and animals without fail, adapting through all the seasons. The work of a farmer is to keep nature under control—not an easy task, but the reward is security for his family. Finally, as an athlete, Timothy performed not for his own glory, but in this case to earn glory for God.

My point is that Timothy has a higher purpose for everything he does, which is always to earn. Whether he earns glory, security, or respect, Timothy is the ultimate Earner, always focused on the hard work needed to achieve his currency of choice.

EARNERS I'VE KNOWN

Sally

My client Sally was an Earner whose primary currency was **time**. A self-employed consultant, she kept her focus on ensuring she had as much free **time** as possible for athletic workouts. Her interest in physical fitness was intense, as befits any Earner, and there is nothing wrong with that. However—like with most Earners—her life wasn't balanced.

Earners who work for money to the exclusion of all else tend to sabotage their relationships. In the same way, Sally sabotaged her financial situation by prioritizing athletic pursuits, instead. In fact, she didn't even bother spending time organizing her professional life. With her focus solely on scheduling workouts, healthy meal planning, and competitions, she let her business slip more and more into the red, as time went by. She wanted to be better at running her business, wanted to be organized, wanted to be perfect at everything, but she just couldn't figure out how to manage her time in such a way that all these factors were dealt with.

Although it's characteristic of Earners to want to be organized and efficient about their currency acquisition, that doesn't mean they're necessarily good at it. Just like with anyone, factors can come into play that stand in the way of them realizing the aims of their Financial Nature. Sometimes that intervening factor is nothing more than the Earner's own overwhelming ambition, and this was the case with Sally.

She ran so much—on treadmills, in public parks, on city streets—as part of her workouts, that I couldn't help but wonder if she was, in some way, running away from something, psychologically. Figuring that out was beyond my level of expertise, as I'm not a psychotherapist, but my work does fall somewhat under the very practical banner of "financial therapist."

I knew Sally's strength would be in staying organized, efficient, and predictably productive, so I helped her decide upon a set hourly rate for her work and a monthly monetary goal that covered all necessary expenses (including saving for the future). This way she could continue focusing the rest of the time on the athletic pursuits that were important to her. With those numbers in mind, she determined how many client hours she was willing and able to book each week. If clients wanted more time, she simply allocated those to a different week, so she made just enough money to fulfil her needs while prioritizing the currency of most value to her (time). For an Earner like Sally, getting those numbers on paper and making decisions based upon facts and figures got the best results.

Having mastered her work schedule by looking closely at the numbers, she was also soon able to do the same for her athletic pursuits. Instead of exercising maniacally as if the world was ending tomorrow, Sally started allocating her work-out time in predictable blocks that provided the scientifically recommended time to rest and recuperate needed by all athletes. Emotionally, getting organized relaxed her and eliminated that feeling of "running away from something" that formerly permeated her desperation-fueled workouts.

The Saver

- *Strengths: cautiousness, independence, frugality, heroism*

- *Weaknesses: greed, isolation, martyrdom*

- *Happiness feels: relaxed, secure*

- *Happiest when: being heroic, rescuing others*

SOCIETY'S HEROES ARE often Savers. These individuals enjoy not only saving money but also using their resources to "save" others, be they family members, pets, underserved populations, or the world's environment. When it comes to currency, Savers are frugal and tend to hold onto things longer than others. This can be an advantage when you discover that an investment a Saver made for a newborn baby turned into a lucrative college fund decades later. Savers love predictability and comfort and the sense of relaxation these qualities provide. Although Savers can be heroic in their efforts to save others, they don't do it for the thrill or adventure. Savers are motivated by putting things right so that the world can once again be predictable and comfortable for all.

Savers are steadfast in temperament and predictable in their actions. They don't tend to seek adventure, but should disaster strike, Savers are ready to spring into action to help others with all the resources they have gathered over the years. As such, they tend toward independence. Let's face it: wealthy, heroic, independent people are often admired, so society often holds Savers in high regard.

SAVER MOTIVATIONS

Conserve

SAVERS WITH A MOTIVATION TO PROTECT

Since those motivated to Protect tend to be a type of Saver to begin with, Saver/Protectors double the power of that tendency to save and conserve. Protective Savers will always have an emergency fund and perhaps even a back-up strategy in case that fund gets depleted during a crisis. You can count on Saver/Protectors to cushion their families against financial stress and often against distress associated with other currencies as well. They may not sit down to calculate these savings, though. It's more likely that the Saver/Protector will simply always save as much as possible without any particular goal or end in sight.

While a Saver/Protector will prioritize long-term financial savings, they will also keep mementos of childhood, write to old friends to keep those **relationships** active, and stay organized so that no **time** is wasted. Concurrent with this tendency, Saver/Protectors can often be extremely conservative in their views and lifestyles, as they never want to risk resources, invite change, or ruin the relaxing lifestyle that comes from always having plenty of resources and being prepared for every emergency.

Deserve

SAVERS WITH A MOTIVATION TO MANAGE

Since Managers tend to pay great attention to detail and pursue their interests with methodical purpose, Saver/Managers pursue their Savings the same way. Like Saver/Protectors, they keep money set aside for emergencies, but unlike Protectors, Managers in this situation will be less conservative about their caches of money and goods. Managers are savvy and don't clutch at resources like Protectors, but instead set goals, do the math, and acknowledge when a relevant reward is deserved. A Saver/Manager saving up for a family vacation, for instance, will know when that goal has been achieved, at which point he or she will go ahead and buy the tickets (and travel insurance, of course!) and spend the money exactly as planned. That's something the hoarding-oriented Protector might be loath to do.

When it comes to managing other resources such as time, friendships, and health, Saver/Managers are proficient at staying in touch with friends, getting health check-ups, and keeping their day-timers on point, but typically not to the point of obsession. The Saver/Manager is the more laid-back version of the generally quite conservative Saver.

Diverge

SAVERS WITH A MOTIVATION TO PURSUE

SAVER

Savers with a motivation to Pursue experience the twin desires of wanting to conserve resources while also wanting to pursue opportunities at every turn. Such a person will be curious and mentally active, but always seeking ways to get ahead without spending money—two goals that often diverge on separate paths. That tendency to be of two minds can create a type of cognitive dissonance causing the Saver/Pursuer to feel frequently torn between opposing desires. Consequently, Saver/Pursuers should set up automatic deposits to their savings accounts so that they can rest assured their all-important savings is being taken care of regularly. Otherwise, should they succumb to the temptation to spend surplus income on a new idea, they will typically regret it, igniting that torturous sense of living with conflicting desires.

More than any other Nature, Saver/Pursuers must spend some time figuring out which currencies they prefer to save. Many Savers feel anxious without a significant chunk of money in their savings accounts, but there are also those whose saving nature tends more toward building relationships, health, or time management. Savers, as a rule, can't relax unless they see significant savings piling up, so such people would do well to ensure they are saving in their preferred currencies and using the other currencies to pursue their drive toward the innovative, new, and exciting things of the future.

Pitfalls for Savers

Let's face it, Savers are often hoarders. This can be healthy, such as when one saves for long term goals. For instance, retirement savings is something that really has no end in sight and can be a great outlet for an endless desire to save. But the habit of endless saving can also take a very unhealthy left turn into piling up belongings in every conceivable nook and cranny. Savers might become survivalists, filling the shelves of their bomb shelters with canned goods—not necessarily a bad thing unless it interferes with your ability to live a balanced life.

Savers can ruin their homes with too much hoarding and an unrealistic view of how much stuff a home is designed to hold. This affects entire families and can cause children to grow up in unclean, unhealthy environments. Communities have laws against extreme hoarding for a reason, as this is simply not a healthy expression of the desire to save. In short, Savers must make conscious decisions to channel their Saving tendencies in wise, productive ways in order to prevent these tendencies from getting out of hand.

Savers also have a tendency to be very independent people—super men and women who fly around in their tights and capes looking for people and communities that need to be saved. The side effect of such incredible independence is a tendency to isolate. Savers would do well to remember that **relationship** is one of the currencies that must be nurtured for a healthy life.

Distortion Fields

Savers bump up against Earners on the left side of their distortion field and Investors on the right side. This is one case where it's very clear which direction a healthy Saver should trend. If Savers lean toward the habits of their Earner cousins, they will be falling prey to the tendency to work harder, not smarter. Savers tend to know how to be smart about their money and make the most of it. But if they behave like Earners, they'll find themselves toiling more than necessary, creating a lot of stress—a real hazard when Savers enjoy relaxation so much.

On the other hand, when Savers adopt the habits of the Financial Nature to their right—Investors—they can really maximize their goals. While the typical Saver doesn't have a very sophisticated way of saving, Investors know how to channel resources in ways that produce dividends. Now that's something Savers can really get behind! No matter which of the three Motivations they subscribe to, Savers will always benefit by learning to be more productive and sophisticated about their saving habits, which will make them feel more content, relaxed, and positive.

SAVER

Saver

CHARACTERISTICS CHART

Superpowers	*Preparedness, relaxation, steadfastness, independence, composure, protectiveness, sustainability, frugality, caution*
Weaknesses	*Isolation, hoarding, greed, penny pinching, enabling*
Keywords	*Save, relax, stability, protection, reserve, caution, isolate, steadiness, safety, economy, gather, collect, accumulate, frugal, gluttony*
Paired With	*Relaxed Financial State, Proficient Financial Level, fourth chakra. (These pairings are explained in chapters 6 and 7)*
Left Distortion Field	*Tends to work harder, not smarter.*
Right Distortion Field	*Tends to double the savings by investing to create an effortless second income.*

SAVERS YOU'VE HEARD OF

The Saver as a Superhero

The heroic ideal of the Saver Nature is perfectly embodied by any caped crusader with super strength, the ability to fly over the mundane world, and a bold willingness to stand up for the downtrodden. Saver superheroes are depicted in all kinds of popular films and television shows. Whether they transform from mild-mannered ordinary people into super savers of humanity or hide out on distant planets where only other super people reside, they tend to swoop to the rescue whenever a crisis needs their attention. Whether they save with super strength, financial wealth, or a wealth of cultivated **relationships**, they are always at the ready to help others.

SAVER

Savers in Literature

EBINEEZER SCROOGE

Who could forget Ebineezer Scrooge from Charles Dickens' A Christmas Carol? The most hated miser who ever lived in a Dickensian universe, he is forced to confront the consequences of his Saver/Protector nature with visits to Christmas past, present, and future. Having turned to the Saver's dark side and become a grouchy hoarder with no love for humanity, Scrooge eventually sees the error of his ways. Although one hopes it never comes to the point of having to face the image of Jacob Marley's ghost in chains, every Saver needs a friend to remind him or her that there is more to life than saving money. In the end, Scrooge learns to balance out his money-saving nature by adding the currency of **relationship** to his wealth.

Savers in History

J. PAUL GETTY

Getty's shrewd deal-making skills began in the Oklahoma oil fields in the early 1920s and led to a level of wealth matched only by Howard Hughes. By 1968, their fortunes were tied at $2 billion. An art collector, Getty founded an eponymously named museum in Los Angeles. Upon his death in 1976, when Getty was considered the world's richest man, The Getty Museum received an endowment that made it the richest museum in the world; however, Getty's legacy of bounty and charity was scarred by miserliness.

In 1973, one of his grandsons was kidnapped, but Getty refused to pay the $17 million ransom, reasoning that if he paid it for that grandchild, he'd have to pay the same for each of his grandchildren and could scarcely afford it. When the kidnappers cut off one of the child's ears, Getty bargained them down to $2.2 million, as that was the maximum payment that would be tax deductible.

Savers in the Bible

Noah is the ultimate Saver. In fact, in the Bible, he literally saves the world. He could have hoarded by filling his ark with every animal he could find, but Noah approached the coming flood methodically, instead. He built a sturdy ark with stables and other appropriate facilities and took only two, and exactly two, of each and every animal on Earth. When the flood was over, Noah released the animals in order to repopulate the planet. He was a wise and frugal Saver/manager who kept a clear head—neither isolating himself with too much independence nor hoarding his savings indiscriminately.

SAVERS I'VE KNOWN

Katie

Katie and her husband George were clients of mine who eventually retired with a nice tidy nest egg. Katie's job for decades had been to function as the family saver. Among other talents, she was a coupon clipper extraordinaire and a master budgeter. George sometimes called her the "soup nazi" after Seinfeld's famous character because she would never let the family budget go over but instead declare, "We can't afford that this month! No soup for you! Not today!"

Her budgeting skills stood the couple in good stead, and when they retired, they did so with plenty of savings. Trouble was, retirement meant there was no longer "savable" money coming in from a paycheck. Instead, the money was coming in as a second income earned from investments, and at this stage of their lives, the goal was no longer to save. Now, the goal was to spend within a fixed budget.

This threw Katie for a loop. Her job as family saver had become obsolete. She experienced a complete identity crisis, but I was able to help her transition her saving tendency into another avenue by explaining that she could now focus on getting bargains with their retirement income instead of saving for retirement itself. At this point in life, there was no longer any point in saving as much as possible. They had achieved their reward for having done that so very well and now had to transition into a new (hopefully more enjoyable) lifestyle.

When taking the Financial Nature assessment, you probably noticed that the very first question asks, "Where do you go to save?" Some people save money in the bank while others save by spending less for their groceries and other staples. A typical Saver will save money in the bank pretty-much forever. But a wise financial planner understands that at different points in your financial life, it actually makes sense to change the ways that you save. This is one example where a couple graduated from one type of savings, then needed to learn to save in a different way. Part four of this book (about Financial States) will teach you how to determine when you need to change strategies like Katie and George did.

Alicia

Alicia is another interesting case of a Saver. An elderly woman with quite a bit of savings, Alicia put me in charge of making sure she didn't run out of money before she died. She would ask her doctor periodically for a measure of her life expectancy, then ask me, "How many years do I have to live, financially?" It was my job to budget her money for the expected number of remaining years.

She had a pension, long-term care policy, and social security, and while her doctor said her body was healthy enough that she could live to be a hundred, she also had the beginnings of dementia, so her life expectancy was a moving target at which her doctor and I both had to guess. Meanwhile, her Saver nature tended toward extremes. After a lifetime of wise saving and investing, Alicia was now very generous to people, more-so than her finances could really handle. In fact, her friends called her a martyr and said she was trying to save the world in the remaining years of her life … at the risk of her own livelihood.

Alicia's money was invested up to level seven, the point of Inductivity (you'll read more on the Financial Levels in chapter six), so in the end, she suffered from Insufficiency in the currency of **health** long before her finances faced Insufficiency. As I helped her, I felt glad that after having saved her money for so long, she got a chance to play out her desire to save others. Knowing Savers, I understand how important this aspect of their Nature is, psychologically.

Alicia's daughter ended up taking care of her in her final months, and the fact that **health** was the only currency lacking helped the family quite a bit.

SAVER

The Investor

- *Strengths: creativity, innovation, intelligence*

- *Weaknesses: erratic/risky behavior, selfishness, thrill seeking*

- *Happiness feels: thrilling, joyful*

- *Happiest when: creating something new*

INVESTORS ARE BIG-PICTURE thinkers. Intelligent and creative, if they don't find something readymade to satisfy their needs, they'll invent or build it themselves. Leaning toward creativity and innovation in everything they do, Investors will risk everything for their ideas. This risk-taking personality never shirks at investing currency if it seems worthwhile. Investors are gamblers and visionaries. Sometimes the rest of the world can't keep up with their out-of-the-box thinking … or so they believe. Financially, Investors have a natural affinity for investing currency in ways that yield dividends.

Investors also like to invest in health, relationship, and time currencies, always using their sharp intellects to improve upon the situation at hand, always cognizant of the balance between risk and reward. Earning or saving steadily, bit by bit, is not good enough for Investors. They prefer to earn their money in big chunks and dramatic ways. Taking risks like this can affect relationships and personal security to a great degree, so Investors must surround themselves with others who are tolerant of their lifestyle choices. When their innovations and investments are successful, this is easy, but when unsuccessful, Investors won't change their modus operandi, and that's when they learn which friends will stick with them through thick and thin. Win or lose, Investors always look at the big picture, always innovate, and never settle for the status quo.

INVESTOR MOTIVATIONS

Indemnify

INVESTORS WITH A MOTIVATION TO PROTECT

Investors motivated by a desire to Protect tend to tamp down some of the riskier aspects of this Financial Nature. Protectors are naturally conservative while Investors take risks, so this combination prompts investments oriented toward providing insurance, or indemnity, of all kinds. Keen to make bets, Investor/Protectors are also careful to hedge those bets with emergency funds and other back-up plans while always investing their savings in ways that yield dividends.

Wise Investor/Protectors set aside time and energy to build their rela-tionships and health, as well. Rather than relying on one big gesture or a burst of erratic energy to increase these currencies, they steadily contribute to these stockpiles—in between creative endeavors, of course—with kind gestures, healthy dietary choices, and ever-present back-up plans just in case that idea to build a better mousetrap doesn't actually pan out. Having backup plans makes Investor/Protectors more likely to succeed.

Diversify

INVESTORS WITH A MOTIVATION TO MANAGE

Investor/Managers have quick minds that are always calculating the risk/reward of each of their big ideas. As Investors, they are prone to taking great leaps of faith, but somewhere along the line, logic is present, too. Rather than relying on back-up plans to insure their risks like Protectors do, Managers tend to rely on diversification, instead. If you have enough innovative irons in the fire, reason Investor/Managers, one of them is sure to succeed! Knowing that they always need money for their big ideas, Investor/Managers will be prone not just to save but to invest with a view to earning that all-important second income.

Investor/Managers view their **relationships** the same way. Rather than relying on one group of friends or business partners, Investor/Managers are more likely to diversify and associate with a wide variety of people. Unlikely to allow themselves to be buttonholed as one particular type of artist, scientist, or innovator, Investor/Managers believe in their own ability to do anything they put their mind to. Pretty soon, others see their infinite potential, too.

Amplify

INVESTORS WITH A MOTIVATION TO PURSUE

Investors are risk takers, as are those with a Motivation to Pursue, so when you put these two traits together, you amplify the no-holds-barred creativity to which the Investor Nature is prone. Investor/Pursuers indulge their wildly innovative minds without doubting themselves. More cautious types may try to hold back Investor/Pursuers, asking them to "be reasonable!" but they won't succeed. Fish gotta swim. Birds gotta fly. Investor/Pursuers gotta create. One day, this person may be sitting quietly hatching an idea, and the next he or she has bought a truck full of materials and is hard at work building a rocket-ship to the moon. You just never know what to expect from Investor/Pursuers, who march to their own drummers. Investor/Pursuers are just as likely to invest their **time** as their money for long-term gains. It just depends upon which currency that individual values most.

Never known for great **time** management, Investor/Pursuers will always be challenged by a hatred of routine and a self-centered nature that makes them forget the birthdays of friends and relations while obsessed with their latest project. Taking time to build **health** and **relationship** currencies, manage their money, and schedule their **time** present great challenges for Investor/Pursuers, but in the meantime, they might just innovate society in a way more balanced people could never do.

PITFALLS FOR INVESTORS

For any gambler, there is always a risk of losing big. Investors are keenly aware of this but simply can't hold themselves back from wanting to "go big or go home." The tendency to speculate can lead Investors to a life of addiction and selfishness. They often think of their risky behaviors as "the last big risk before I make it big!" but can end up pursuing one crazy scheme after another, ad infinitum. It's fun to associate with Investors because of their thrill-seeking personalities but even that can wear on people's nerves after a while. Investors are those people you point to as geniuses and iconoclasts, but you don't always want to hang out with them and often don't understand them. Their intensity and unusual ways of thinking can lead to isolation.

DISTORTION FIELDS

When we talk about living in the eye of a hurricane, never is this more apt than when we talk about the creative Investor. When Investors step away from their usual modus operandi, they tend to bump up against either the Saver Nature on the left or the Lever Nature on the right. Savers are a lot more relaxed by nature than Investors, and they tend to be prepared and frugal and generally more cautious in their behavior, so it may seem like having Investors lean toward being Savers would be a good, calming influence on them. But, as we've learned in our study of distortion fields, it's always wise to head toward adopting the traits of the Nature to your right, not left. Here's why: Every Financial Nature seeks equilibrium and can only achieve this by moving forward toward creation of something new, toward the future, not back toward the past.

For an Investor, behaving like the staid, conservative Saver would squelch creativity and innovation. Bursts of creative energy are needed to spawn new ideas. So, while the Saver will benefit from taking on the innovative qualities of the Investor, Investors will not benefit from relaxing like Savers.

Instead, they should learn some of the qualities of the even-more-innovative Lever. Levers know how to leverage their creativity to achieve more with less work, help more people with less money, and generally channel creative energy into systems. So, while an Investor might build one rocket-ship to the moon, a Lever can teach her how to distribute rocket-ship kits that give the whole world access to this new technology.

INVESTOR

Investor CHARACTERISTICS CHART

Superpowers	*Creativity, drive, productivity, innovation, inventiveness, intelligence, charm, enjoyment*
Weaknesses	*Speculation, addiction, erratic behavior, greed, selfishness, risky behavior, thrill-seeking, gambling*
Keywords	*Action, thrill, joy, profit, daring, enthusiasm, accomplishment, creativity, harvesting*
Paired With	*Create Financial State, Productive Financial Level, fifth chakra. (These pairings are explained in chapters 6 and 7)*
Left Distortion Field	*Tends to tamp down creativity.*
Right Distortion Field	*Tends to harness creativity into replicable systems.*

INVESTOR

INVESTORS YOU'VE HEARD OF

The Investor as a Superhero

Popular culture is chock full of billionaire superhero types who innovate their own super-heroic skills. With endless access to the best technology available, these bold individuals don't have heroism thrust upon them but seek it out. They invent their own bulletproof suits, design their own high-speed vehicles, and build their own high-tech centers of innovation. Typically functioning with a sidekick or two who takes care of all the mundane aspects of super-heroism, these big personalities are always brilliant innovators who stop at nothing to achieve their big-picture goals for a better society.

Investors in History

BENJAMIN FRANKLIN

One of America's most influential founding fathers, Franklin is known for being a polymath, or someone whose knowledge spans numerous disciplines. This famous scholar invented the lightning rod, bifocals, the Franklin Stove, swim fins, a urinary catheter, and a musical instrument called an Armonica. He refused to patent any of these ideas, as he felt such tools should be shared freely. America's first ambassador to France, he also served as postmaster and governor and made a mark as an early abolitionist, proponent of vegetarianism, and chess player. Franklin founded a couple of newspapers, a fire department, and a university as well as famously helping develop the ideals behind the US Constitution.

It isn't necessarily true that an Investor is also an inventor, but the agile, creative mind of Benjamin Franklin is a perfect example of the type of person likely to fall under the Financial Natures as an Investor. Ironically, Franklin's portrait graces America's hundred-dollar bill.

GEORGE SOROS AND WARREN BUFFET

Soros and Buffet stand out as two of the world's most famous Investors in the most literal sense of the term. Soros was a short-term speculator who founded the aggressive and successful Soros Fund Management hedge fund. Meanwhile, Warren Buffet, often called "the Oracle of Omaha," amassed a multibillion-dollar company by buying stocks and companies through Berkshire Hathaway. They are, quite literally, perfect examples of those who understand the many benefits and intricacies of investing.

Investors in the Bible

Because the Investor Financial Nature is so creative, the best comparison from the Bible is God himself. The ultimate creator, God famously created Heaven and Earth, the animals, plants, and people, and then he rested. When we get to part four of this book, where we talk about Financial States, you'll see why it's crucial for an Investor to go through all seven States in order to achieve a goal. Exclusively for the Investor, the seventh state is rest and relaxation, allowing such people to recuperate before their next wildly creative endeavor.

INVESTORS I'VE KNOWN

Harry

Harry was a client who took the assessment and proved himself to be an Investor. I had lunch with him one day and he asked me to elaborate on my theory about how our feelings and instincts play a large role in how we approach finances.

"You took the assessment and got 'Investor,' right? So, my guess is that your savings is invested?" I asked.

"Yes, of course," he replied.

"All of it?" I asked.

He replied that it was, and he had very little in a readily accessible savings account.

"So, here's a little mental exercise," I said. "Imagine taking ten percent of your investments and putting it in a savings account."

"Holy crap!" he said. "The hair on the back of my neck just stood up!"

"So you had an emotional reaction to that," I countered. "Can you relax into the idea and make that emotional reaction go away, for now?"

He said he could.

I said, "Okay, now take another ten percent of your investments and put that also in the savings account."

He said he had the same visceral reaction to the idea the second time.

"Do you see?" I asked. "You are wired to prefer your money be invested rather than sitting around not doing anything. You're thinking, 'What's the utility of having money just sitting there?' But here's what you don't realize: due to the volatile nature of the economy, it's always possible your investments could drop twenty, thirty, even forty percent in value. If that happens, what happens to the value of your savings? It goes up by that amount, relatively speaking. If a recession comes along, the value of your investments drop, but the value of your cash savings increases. Not only that, but under those circumstances, you can take some of your savings and buy valuable investments at rock bottom prices. Do you see how cash positions you for recovery from economic events? That's why saving is important, not just investing. You think of your emotional reaction toward investing and away from saving as logical, but it's not. It's emotional."

Harry chewed on that information for quite a while!

Marcus

My friend Marcus had the brilliant mind of an Investor but experienced difficulty with some of life's more mundane tasks. For instance, he always bought terrible, used cars that broke down all the time. This made it difficult for him to hold down a steady job or be reliable at all. Not a rich man, he continued this pattern, going from car to car and job to job for quite some time, thinking there was no way out of his troubles.

Finally, I sat down with him and looked at his finances. I was able to show him that if he leased a reliable four-wheel-drive vehicle, he'd never have to worry about breaking down by the side of the road again, no matter the weather, and could therefore commence to seriously build a career.

The $250 monthly price tag seemed high until Marcus considered the accumulated costs of the repairs needed on his clunkers, plus the additional benefit of reliable income that would both be enabled by the car and enable him to have the car, in turn.

His emotional relationship with buying clunkers was based in, first of all, not valuing his own worth. Secondly, it represented a type of false hope: with every clunker, he was influenced by the low price and an eternal optimism that told him it would never break down. Marcus always convinced himself this next car was a real bargain.

Once he looked at the numbers, Marcus understood that his fantasies about the benefits of buying used cars were not based in reality. He needed a reliable vehicle as a tool to further his career, just as a carpenter needs a hammer. When he finally leased the vehicle, Marcus experienced the thrill of investing in himself, perhaps for the first time, and never looked back.

Marcus hadn't really come into his own as an Investor yet, financially, but he had the Investor's big-picture, creative mindset. This type of mind can make someone brilliant, but there is danger, too. Investors like Marcus sometimes lack the practical viewpoints found in the more grounded Financial Natures.

The Lever

- *Strengths: cooperation, helpfulness, supportiveness, synergy*

- *Pitfalls: selfish, manipulative, exploitative, lazy, unrealistic, insular*

- *Happiness feels: easy, stress-free*

- *Happiest when: uplifting self and others*

A LEVER IS A tool that makes it easy to lift a heavy object. As such, Levers like to find ways to make life easier and more productive for themselves and others. A naturally cooperative Financial Nature, the Lever enjoys building systems and structures that increase productivity of all kinds. Because they are highly motivated to make life stress-free, this often means delegating mundane or repetitive tasks to others. Levers are master delegators. If your car breaks down, a hard-working Earner would get a set of wrenches and fix it, a heroic Saver would produce the money to rescue it from the scrap heap, but a Lever would have it towed and repaired as well as set up automated oil changes, tire rotations, and trouble-shooting appointments between you and a local mechanic to ensure you never have a breakdown again. The Lever might also arrange to purchase a warranty to make payments easier. Levers see life's mission as a search for elevation and enlightenment. Naturally helpful Levers want to find better ways of doing things so that every aspect of life is easier, not just for themselves but for those around them.

In finance, "leveraging" is a matter of borrowing money in order to invest it and get a healthy return on that investment. No matter whether Levers are dog walkers, business owners, or physicists, they use this same principle in everything they do. They are unafraid to borrow or spend on anything likely to yield a profit, and that accounts for the currencies of **time, relationship,** and **health** as well as **stuff.** For example, saying no to lower-priority activities allows Levers to "borrow" **time** they can invest in higher-priority activities. Levers are adept at analyzing life's choices and consciously making such trade-offs, always with a view to reducing stress. Levers naturally understand something called the "positive multiplier effect," which means that when you spend currency the right way, the benefits you receive far outweigh your investment.

LEVER MOTIVATIONS

Delegate
LEVERS WITH A MOTIVATION TO PROTECT

LEVER

Levers are risk takers who enjoy making trade-offs to produce a desired effect, whether it be financial gain or a chance to spend more time with their loved ones. Those motivated to Protect eliminate that element of risk by setting up systems to ensure safety and security to elevate their family's **health** and finances long into the future. Typically, this means delegating responsibilities to either computerized systems or human experts. Lever/Protectors automate their bill paying and savings to make life easy and systematic. Their sense of enlightenment comes from having set up a life that provides for everyone in their family (and perhaps community) with maximum ease and minimum work.

Lever/Protectors try to ensure the health of their **relationships** by setting aside time and energy to make family life just as easy as their work life. As with everything, they want to succeed here with the least amount of stress. They see life as a matter of trading one thing for another with a view to seeking win/win solutions both in daily decision-making and big-picture life decisions. For them, no goal is impossible but simply a matter of working out what assets are no longer needed and can be sacrificed to achieve new goals.

Coordinate

LEVERS WITH A MOTIVATION TO MANAGE

Levers motivated by Management have active minds that are always looking for new opportunities to leverage assets toward a more enlightened way of life. Eternally seeking to create ease and simplicity through systematic thought and action, Lever/Managers don't stop at providing basic comfort, as Protectors are wont to do, but tend to seek new ideas for **time** saving, **stuff** saving, and **health** improvement measures that reduce stress on both small and large scales.

Once Lever/Managers have created systems that make their own lives easy, they'll reach out to coordinate with their communities or underserved populations in the world at large, always seeking to find that brilliant invention that brings water to the desert or food to the starving. Then, Lever/Managers figure out how to get that asset from supplier to user by leveraging assets. Borrowing money is never off the table, as Lever/Managers have a keen, big-picture mindset willing and able to calculate the benefits of such investments for the long term and derive ways to pay the costs in the meantime.

LEVER

Educate

LEVERS WITH A MOTIVATION TO PURSUE

When the naturally forward-looking Lever Nature is paired with a motivation to Pursue, change is always on the horizon. Lever/Pursuers are big-idea, big-picture people who thrive at developing systems to improve lives and are eager to help others elevate their situations. Yet Lever/Pursuers pay little attention to detail as they charge forward. Often bursting with bold ideas, they can trip over their own ambitions. As such, the ability to delegate is key to the success of Lever/Pursuers who need more detail-oriented personalities that can dot the I's and cross the T's to ensure their proposals succeed.

When it comes to **health, time,** and **relationship** currencies, Lever/ Pursuers seek the same systematic, stress-free lifestyles as all other Levers but are typically less practical than Managers and Protectors. These individuals tend to always have a new iron in the fire, a new problem to solve by making brilliant trade-offs. As with everything in life, not every trade or risk turns out the way one expects, so there is likely to be more volatility in the lives of Lever/Pursuers, but that is paired with a lot of satisfaction at all their accomplishments.

PITFALLS FOR LEVERS

Because Levers always seek to make life easier and more stress-free, they can be selfish and, frankly, lazy. When too ambitious, Levers can also over-leverage by taking on debt they can't repay. At their worst, Levers may manipulate or exploit others in order to facilitate their naturally opportunistic ways. Easily frustrated when forced into situations where hard or uninspiring work is involved, Levers can be hard to work with unless they are in a position to take the lead.

With their naturally community-oriented nature and innate desire to create a better world, Levers stuck in dead-end situations will never stop trying to borrow or leverage other assets in order to get ahead. This tendency can be an asset, but if surrounded by the unimaginative and unambitious, Levers will be made to feel different and could descend into depression. Giving in to entropy is not in a Lever's skill set.

DISTORTION FIELDS

The eye of the Lever's hurricane stands equidistant between that of Investor and Giver. If trending left, toward the Investor, Levers will bring out their more creative and productive side. The trouble is that creative people like Investors can seldom successfully delegate their work, as the very nature of creativity is entirely dependent upon one's own imagination. Because Levers love to delegate and hate to work hard, they'll be frustrated taking on all the extra work entailed in the role of an Investor.

If leaning toward the generous, intuitive traits of a Giver, Levers will work with enhanced leadership qualities to bring their systematic ideas to life. Like community-oriented Levers, Givers always seek out the best workers and smartest organizers to ensure positive social change, so if Levers are to leave the center of their tendencies, the eye of their hurricane, it's best for them to lean toward the traits of a Giver, which can supplement their already activism-oriented Nature.

LEVER

Lever   CHARACTERISTICS CHART

Superpowers	*cooperation, connection, helpfulness, self-awareness, team building, seeking synergy, seeking enlightenment and ease*
Weaknesses	*selfishness, laziness, manipulativeness, exploitativeness, unrealistic expectations, insularity*
Keywords	*leverage, ease, enlightenment, relationship, contribution, reciprocation, levity, symbiosis, cooperation, help, opportunity, lift, raise, elevate*
Paired With	*Elevate Financial State, Deductive Financial Level, sixth chakra. (These pairings are explained in chapters 6 and 7)*
Left Distortion Field	*Tends to work harder than desired.*
Right Distortion Field	*Tends toward enhanced cooperation with others for community benefit.*

LEVER

Levers You've Heard Of

The Lever as a Superhero

When we think of superheroes in popular mythology, we often imagine lone wolves, those who seek to single-handedly save people and communities from evil villains, but the Lever stands outside that pack. Instead, the Lever can be compared to the type of superhero whose strength is in wisdom, diplomacy, and nurturing. Often female, these superheroes display fierce martial skills paired with the ability to manage a league of other "lone wolf" types. Because her skill lies in delegating tasks, she is an excellent leader of an organized system that dispatches the various supers to where their super skills are ideally suited.

Levers in History

DR. MARTIN LUTHER KING JR.

The most visible spokesperson for the American civil rights movement from 1955 until his assassination in 1968, Dr. Martin Luther King Jr. understood that a better relationship between the races in America could be achieved by leveraging the significant power of large numbers of individuals united in a common cause. Striving for voting rights, desegregation, and labor rights, he oversaw nonviolent demonstrations such as the 1955 Montgomery Bus Boycott, the 1963 March on Washington, and two of the three 1965 Selma-to-Montgomery Marches. After winning the Nobel Peace Prize, Dr. King expanded his organization to include opposition to poverty, exploitative capitalism, and the Vietnam War.

A master in the art of leverage with the Lever's typical goal of seeking enlightenment and upliftment for the masses, Dr. King "borrowed" the time of thousands of activists in order to "invest" in a mass uprising that would garner support in the form of votes from Americans and their elected representatives who shared these ideals. With his famous speeches and nonviolent actions, Dr. King maximized the inter-racial relationship currency of all Americans.

LEVER

MOHAMMED YUNUS

A Bangladeshi economics professor, Mohammed Yunus invented the concept of microlending in 1976. Having recognized that many uneducated, rural populations were being exploited by loan sharks, Yunus offered these people small, unsecured loans at reasonable rates. His first loan of just $27 was to a community of women whose sole source of income came from the art of weaving bamboo stools. Because their handicraft required initial investment and they operated with no financial margin, the community had previously borrowed from exploitative organizations and was thus mired in poverty, only making a penny per stool.

With Yunus' lending system, however, this long-suffering community managed to leverage its significant organizational and creative skill to take charge of its business once and for all. Yunus' genius was in understanding how very little financial leverage developing-world communities like this needed in order to completely transform peoples' lives. He also understood that the risk incurred in helping them was relatively insignificant to the developed world. By inventing microlending, he helped the underprivileged enjoy the same leveraging power as the highly educated.

Levers in the Bible

Abraham is a good example of a Lever in the Bible. A master negotiator and diplomat, he always worked to improve **relationships** between people. For instance, his nephew Lot lived with him for a time, but when things became tense, it was clear that Lot needed to find his own way. Diplomatically, Abraham gave a piece of choice land to Lot, enabling him to save face and get off to a good start in life.

In the book of Genesis, Abraham also uses his powerful mediation skills to convince God to save the son of Sodom. But the thing Abraham is best known for is the willingness to sacrifice his son Isaac when asked to do so by God. With little Isaac poised to be killed, God saw Abraham's total dedication and servitude, so he stopped the sacrifice and saved the boy. Gruesome as this story may be, Abraham understood that his relationship with God was the greatest bargaining chip anyone could ever have, so if he had to sacrifice something in order to maximize that currency, it would be worth it in the end.

LEVERS I'VE KNOWN

Clara and Kaylee

I work with a group dedicated to civic leadership, where nonprofits and businesspeople learn about each other and develop strategies to better serve their communities. That's where I met Clara and Kaylee, who ran a foundation to support the arts. After listening to people from all walks of life participate in a brainstorming session meant to help them with their goals, I saw the two of them looking more confused than ever. I pulled Clara and Kaylee aside, said, "I know exactly what your problem is," and offered to take them to lunch.

"You're an Investor," I said to Kaylee. "You're the idea person." I asked her for some of her ideas, and she rattled off eight different highly creative, inspiring ideas.

"You're a Lever," I said to Clara. "You're a skilled manager who can uplift the entire organization with your systematic organizing." Then I turned back to Kaylee, the creative mastermind, and asked, "Which of your ideas has the most promise?" She selected one. "Which has the least?" I asked. She selected another. Finally, I asked, "Do you think the first idea would be more successful if you mothballed that second idea and put all the energy into the one?" She agreed that it would. Next, I asked, "Do you have an employee who is currently putting energy into the second idea that could be repurposed into the first idea?"

Her answer was no. It was only the two of them at the organization, and they were both big-picture thinkers. You see, part of their problem was that when Clara, the creative Investor, assigned a project to Kaylee, Kaylee, being a managerial type, wanted to delegate the nuts and bolts of the job to someone else. But nobody else was there.

I explained that too many chefs were spoiling this broth. They needed a different personality type in the mix. That person should be a hard worker who enjoyed getting into the trenches with the nitty gritty of what needed to be done. While Clara and Kaylee were both brilliant, neither would ever thrive at that type of task. So, they saved money by narrowing down their eight endeavors to the three most likely to succeed, then hired someone who took the Financial Natures assessment and was shown to be an Earner. With these three personality types in the mix, the organization would be able to achieve its newly limited goals much more effectively. Thus, they could grow, step-by-step, to the level where eventually their organization could actually handle eight projects at once.

The Giver

- ➤ *Strengths: generosity, leadership, teaching, helping, gratitude*

- ➤ *Pitfalls: martyrdom, enabling, fantasizing, lack of self care*

- ➤ *Happiness feels: fulfilling*

- ➤ *Happiest when: giving to others*

As THE NAME implies, Givers are motivated by service to others and making the world a better place. With their strong sense of spirituality, Givers tend to be leaders and visionaries. This Financial Nature is intuitive and able to enter a "flow" state, tuning in to a deep way of processing information not available to all.

With their high-minded notions and belief in the power of positive thought and action, Givers operate on a level that more practical, self-centered Financial Natures can't fathom. Viewing the world in terms of paths to enlightenment means Givers work not to enrich themselves but with a sense that a rising tide lifts all boats. This view of the world can make them enlightened, but it can also lead to naiveté and a lack of practicality in decision making. Most Givers would agree the trade-off is worth it, however, for they take pleasure in their ability to see the world selflessly. For a Giver, happiness lies in a sense of deep fulfillment.

GIVER MOTIVATIONS

Save

GIVERS WITH A MOTIVATION TO PROTECT

Givers who are motivated to Protect want to save the world with an emphasis on protecting it from harm rather than pushing it forward toward enlightenment. They identify threats on the horizon and work to provide all safety measures necessary to keep danger from their loved ones and the world at large. This is the least visionary of the Giver types and the most careful. Other Givers may be more optimistic and likely to follow huge, world-shaping visions, but Giver/Protectors do their saving from the point of view of pessimism. Their mission is to keep an eye out for the forces of evil, the dark clouds on the horizon, and to do what it takes to save their communities from them.

Drive

GIVERS WITH A MOTIVATION TO MANAGE

Giver/Managers seek ways to save the world, then work out all the details in order to make it happen. If life is an Academy Award winning film, Giver/Managers are the actor/director/producers. They have the vision and drive to create a movement with deep meaning and significance, compute every detail of that movement, and make the connections necessary to take the idea to the highest level. The only trouble is that Givers don't tend to be great at delegating, so there is always the danger that over-achieving Giver/Managers will take on too much and simply collapse before the film goes into post-production. However, Giver/Managers, with their people skills, are the Givers most likely to be able to develop the skill of delegating, so such people should focus on improving this innate weakness first and foremost.

GIVER

GIVERS WITH A MOTIVATION TO PURSUE

Givers motivated to Pursue never stop dreaming and trying. These socially active individuals are likely to be found volunteering for every worthy cause in town, sometimes overbooking themselves as they reach out to everyone in need. Giver/Pursuers may chase their altruistic dreams overseas, becoming adventurous doctors, teachers, and others who serve refugees all over the world. For Giver/Pursuers, too much giving is never enough, and they can become emotionally overburdened with other peoples' problems. At that point, the challenge for them is to be able to be the recipient of help that they desperately need, and that's difficult for all Givers, especially the ultra-active Giver/Pursuer.

PITFALLS FOR GIVERS

Givers are buoyed by the joy of helping others—a wonderful trait much needed in the world. At the same time, their need to help others can also be self-serving. After all, when your sense of self-worth revolves around your ability to help others, sometimes the work you do is selfishly motivated. What appears to be altruistic on the outside may be a bandage over an inner lack or deep insecurity. Tied to that is a tendency for Givers to try to solve problems by giving people what the Giver thinks they need rather than what the recipient actually needs or wants. This is controlling behavior disguised as altruism, and it shows a certain dark side to the Giver.

Even when Givers' motivations are pure, they can drive themselves to exhaustion and become martyrs for their causes, whether they mean to or not. Motivated to achieve, Givers tend to take the bulk of their work upon themselves but would often be better served by developing skills around collaboration and delegation to fulfil their worthy goals.

GIVER

DISTORTION FIELDS

Swirling between the Lever on the left and the Taker on the right, Givers can be drawn in two very different directions when they flow outside the eye of their hurricane. Levers are systems-thinkers who strive to make life easier and more stress free. When Givers lean in this direction, their tendency to give to others can become systematized. There is nothing inherently wrong with that, as Levers do it all the time, but Givers require a leadership role paired with the ability to conduct their business intuitively. Systems and structures tend to rub Givers the wrong way after some time, and they'll swirl in their hurricane to the other side. Over on the right, Givers encounter the Taker Financial Nature where they feel an immediate affinity for the intuitive side of life. Like Takers, Givers benefit from being in touch with their intuition and instincts. When Givers are motivated to react like Takers, it is usually for the good of all rather than for selfish reasons. Givers leaning toward the Taker Nature are moving forward toward an even greater ability to give.

Giver   CHARACTERISTICS CHART

Superpowers	*Generosity, leadership, teaching, intuitive flow, helping, healing, gratitude, sharing, vision, positivity*
Weaknesses	*Martyrdom, enabling, living in a dream world, lack of self-care*
Keywords	*Give, passion, evolve, intuit, visionary, leadership, generous, flow, extrasensory, generous, charitable, abundance, thoughtful, gratitude, enrichment*
Paired With	*Lead Financial State, Inductive Financial Level, seventh chakra. (These pairings are explained in chapters 6 and 7)*
Left Distortion Field	*Tends to fall into systems thinking and away from intuition.*
Right Distortion Field	*Trending toward using intuitive/ reactive qualities more.*

GIVER

GIVERS YOU'VE HEARD OF

The Giver as a Superhero

With its deep connection to spirituality, the Giver Financial Nature is the type of superhero that uses little-understood powers such as psychic skills, telekinesis, and telepathy to execute visionary projects that save individuals and communities in a grand way. Not content to save kittens from being stuck in trees or individuals from evil doers, the Giver superhero is the type that saves an entire country from a typhoon by stopping the waves with the power of his mind. The Giver is the superhero who saves the whole planet from a speeding comet destined to usher in a new ice age by shifting the planetary orbit through its spiritual connection with the universe. In short, if the Giver is a superhero, it's one with a connection to supernatural forces outside the ken of ordinary mortals. What's more, the Giver is powered not by love for any individual but by love for all of humanity.

Givers in History

THICH NHAT HANH

Zen master, global spiritual teacher, peace activist, and poet, Thich Nhat Hanh's primary message was that through mindfulness, people can learn to be happy in the present moment and build peace in the world. Thich Nhat Hanh founded the Engaged Buddhism movement during the Vietnam War when many Vietnamese monks and nuns faced a quandary: should they continue the contemplative life in their monasteries or help their countrymen suffering so greatly from war? Thich Nhat Hanh didn't hesitate to reach out to help others and eventually became a pioneer in bringing Buddhism's peaceful message to the West.

Thich Nhat Hanh found new ways to teach mindful breathing, walking, and living that made Buddhist practice available to beginners. His teachings include mindful consumption, mindful **relationships**, and ethical livelihood, and are predicated upon the notion that true daily mindfulness is not a path to achievement but to inner happiness.

GIVER

A scholar, teacher, and activist, Thich Nhat Hanh decided the typically reclusive life of a Bodhisattva was not for him. Instead, he chose to become a leader, and eventually his lectures filled stadiums. He founded a Buddhist University in Saigon, A Buddhist publishing house, a peace activist magazine, and a new order of Buddhism called the Order of Interbeing. When Dr. Martin Luther King Jr. nominated Thich Nhat Hanh for the Nobel Peace Prize, he called him "an apostle of peace and nonviolence."

ECKHART TOLLE

Best known for his first book, New York Times best-selling *The Power of Now*, Eckhart Tolle is a non-denominational spiritual guide, counselor, and author who claims Buddhism, Hinduism, and Christianity as his influences. Now famous for his association with Oprah Winfrey, with whom he has conducted numerous webinars, Tolle experienced suicidal depression in his youth leading to an intense spiritual awakening at the age of 29, when he recalls having achieved enlightenment overnight. He has authored *Stillness Speaks* (2003), *A New Earth: Awakening to Your Life's Purpose* (2008), and *Guardians of Being* (2009).

Tolle's teachings center around precepts such as "awareness is the greatest agent for change," which prompt followers to identify and reject their defense mechanisms and tendencies for denial. He advises followers to, instead, sit with and accept their feelings and imperfections. As such, Tolle strives to heal people from society's urge to perfect oneself toward unattainable goals and instead help them strive for awareness and acceptance of reality.

Givers in the Bible

In the Bible, the character of Jesus is the ultimate Giver. He experiences the full range of Giver attributes in that he performs miracles such as healing the sick, driving out evil spirits, calming storms on the sea, feeding the masses, raising the dead, and the famous incident of turning water into wine. In Bible stories, Jesus exists solely to serve and enlighten humanity toward a better way of living, a better philosophy of kindness. Jesus also famously becomes a martyr … some might say the ultimate martyr.

GIVER

In the Bible, Jesus' martyrdom is portrayed as a good thing, but in our daily lives, we typically discourage one another from taking our giving to such an extreme that it kills us or destroys our livelihood. In order to keep on contributing to the world, Givers need to maintain an awareness of how much **time**, **relationship**, **health**, and **stuff** they can realistically give while keeping themselves nourished enough to continue their missions. Jesus faced this challenge, too, and struggled with his urge toward martyrdom, wondering whether he was making his final decision for the right reasons. His struggle sends the message that Givers like himself must individually evaluate their situations and determine how much giving will truly serve a higher purpose.

GIVERS I'VE KNOWN

Olivia and Hannah

I currently serve on the board of directors for an organization that brings yoga to underserved populations. The non-profit was founded by my neighbor and fellow yogi, Olivia. One day, Olivia and I found ourselves in a neighborhood yoga class together. I have a yoga mat printed to look like a ten-dollar bill, because for me, money represents love, groundedness, and mindfulness. Granted, this philosophy is distinct from that of most yoga practitioners, but I gotta be me. When Olivia saw my yoga mat, she was inspired to share a mission with which she had been tasked.

She had recently been to a yoga retreat with Hannah, where they had gone to develop their nonprofit. The program brought yoga to prisoners behind bars, but they wanted to also develop a secondary mission to bring yoga to drug-addiction treatment centers. Hannah and Olivia each came away from the retreat with a resolution to "find someone to help you have a better relationship with money." When she saw my yoga mat, Olivia knew I was that guy. We had lunch together, and the rest is history.

I put Hannah and Olivia through my Currency Camp program, which teaches the principles in this book in a hands-on manner tied directly to one's personal or business finances. At the end of the camp, they realized that as Givers, they needed to balance the relationship between giving and receiving. When running a nonprofit, sometimes you have to ask people for money—a skill they hadn't yet developed, as they had been paying the expenses of the program so far from their own coffers.

Ironically, Hannah's husband, also a Giver, ran a company that built affordable housing—something that actually led to them making such a good living that they had, so far, been able to bankroll the yoga non-profit on surplus alone. In order to expand, though, they had to learn to ask for money, something that's a lot more natural to the Taker, the next Financial Nature after Giver. I needed to teach them to adopt a tendency common to another Nature (just long enough to accomplish a goal). How did I do it? Well, that question is a great lead-in to the next two parts of this book, where I will teach you when, why, and how to do that very thing in order to accomplish your own goals.

Giselle and Tom

It was a Monday morning when I received a call from Giselle. She had heard of our work and thought I was just the person to help her and her husband Tom. She asked for an appointment, and I offered to squeeze her in the following Tuesday. She asked for something sooner, and I said, "This afternoon at two."

She said, "We'll be there!"

When they arrived, we jumped right into the situation. Apparently, Tom had made an offer and put earnest money down on a real estate purchase (a row house in Savannah, Georgia) without first consulting Giselle. They had ten days to back out or risk losing the deposit. Tom believed that this purchase would become part of his legacy and a great retirement investment. At 69, a doctor, and still working, he was having difficulty convincing Giselle.

We had them take our assessment on the spot. Giselle was a Saver and Tom a Giver. With this new awareness, we were able to understand the gap between the Saver and the Giver. Tom, the Giver, was averse to borrowing money. Giselle, the Saver, was uncomfortable with Tom's idea to use all their savings and a fair amount of their investments to buy the Savannah

Row House. Giselle was willing to negotiate and reach some kind of a compromise, but Tom dug in.

We agreed to do a financial plan, gather facts, run projections, and use this fact-based process to help them evaluate alternative purchase plans. Tom and Giselle agreed that if the purchase was less risky—perhaps done a different way—then maybe they could each have what they needed to go forward with confidence.

In the end, the analysis demonstrated the merits of real estate as a means to diversify the portfolio and lower their overall risk profile. However, the idea of this particular real estate purchase was less effective when we realized the expenditure represented too big a piece of their plan. My evaluation of the merits of this purchase was related to how much they had in other investments and how much the real estate purchase would cost relative to their income. Thus, I was able to demonstrate to Tom that liquidating so much of their savings and investments in this way put them at greater risk. Borrowing more for longer would be a better strategy that would make the purchase less risky. In the end, Tom became nervous about borrowing more, so they compromised by buying a less expensive, less grand Savannah row house.

One of the factors in this case was Tom and Giselle's age difference. Tom was thinking legacy at 69, but Giselle was ten years younger, just wondering when Tom would retire. Life stages and age differences are often factors in what causes partners to have different outlooks on money.

GIVER

The Taker

- *Strengths: reactive, instinctive, resourceful*

- *Pitfalls: impulsive, chaotic, panicky*

- *Happiness feels: exciting*

- *Happiest when: taking risks*

IN DESCRIBING THE Taker, I'd like to return to the fact that every human trait is like a coin, where one side represents the beneficial side of that trait, but if you flip it, you can see the dangerous side of the same trait. You could also think of each Nature existing on a continuum.

No matter whether someone is a Zen master or a criminal, I don't like to think of any person as being inherently disordered or superior. Rather, peoples' Natures can manifest in the balanced middle or at either extreme end of the continuum of their personality type. Where the Taker is concerned, this personality runs the gamut from intuitive artist to destructive thief. At its best, the Taker is as instinctive as an animal and therefore has access to a part of the brain more intellectual types simply don't use.

For instance, a musical Taker might have great natural rhythm and perfect pitch. Ask Takers exactly how they sing or play instruments or know when an instrument is in tune, and they probably can't tell you. They just know. Ask athletic Takers how they know when to shoot for a goal or basket or weave to the left or right and, again, they can only say "intuition!" Artists, dancers, even business moguls can be Takers, but what they all have in common is access to a type of instinctive knowing that can't be rationally explained. As such, they tend to use that intuition to make quick decisions and seize opportunities. Intuition doesn't plan ahead, so Takers tend to live in the moment more than most other Natures. Although Takers fly by the seat of their pants, they're also highly motivated to pursue what they want (as opposed to what they need) and this can help them achieve great things.

TAKER MOTIVATIONS

Extraction

TAKERS WITH A MOTIVATION TO PROTECT

Takers with a Motivation to Protect have access to some really valuable tools. Knowing how to use them helps Takers stay on the positive side of the coin that is their personality. Among those tools is the ability to extract value from any given situation or experience. Takers are the people who, if you put them in front of a table piled high with old junk, will reach in and pull out the one valuable antique. In the same way, their intuition guides them to extract the one valuable idea from a business model gone wrong or a random brainstorming session.

Financially, if a group seeks a quick and simple way to stop cash from flowing out or, conversely, to access a quick influx of money, Taker/Protectors are the people to turn to. It is the Taker's quickness of mind paired with the Protector's desire for stability that helps them develop instant solutions, quick patches for problems, and MacGyver-like problem-solving methods. That's the positive side of this Nature. Conversely, don't make Taker/Protectors look bad by turning to them for long-term plans, detailed itineraries, or intellectual analysis.

TAKER

Reaction

TAKERS WITH A MOTIVATION TO MANAGE

Takers are *reactors*, even when they have the motivation of a perfectionistic Manager. They sense problems and react with solutions but don't engage in long explanations as to why their solutions are right. They just know, and if you don't trust their knowing, this will frustrate Takers because they can't usually explain themselves. If you want to drive Taker/Managers crazy, demand a Powerpoint presentation. When it comes to Taker/Managers, if you know them, you trust them. If you don't, they don't have much use for you.

The key to making this reactive personality work at its best is for Taker/Managers to stay confident and continue reacting without judging themselves or getting emotional about the ups and downs of any endeavor. After all, nobody is right all the time, so Takers' intuition can also fail. When this happens, it can lead them (especially if they're perfectionistic Managers) to doubt their reactive nature, and that's doom. Taker/Managers must continue to have faith in themselves, understanding that their reactive tendencies will improve the more they trust and use them.

Interaction

TAKER WITH A MOTIVATION TO PURSUE

When Takers are also Pursuers, their naturally instinctive, spontaneous Natures are doubled. This can maximize Takers' access to that all-important intuition that fuels their lives. Taker/Pursuers rely on their intuitive Natures more readily than Protectors and Managers because they understand, deep down, how this instinctive quality is central to their very being. They are less prone to fall prey to the doubt that mainstream society places on the power of intuition and instinct. Taker/Pursuers don't have the ability to pretend to be like everyone else. They are 100% deeply involved in their intuitive, spontaneous, instinctive way of seeing things and their behavior reflects this. Taker/Pursuers are different by nature. Don't judge them. They might seem

TAKER

weird to the more conservative Natures in society, but when their way of being is nurtured, it gives them access to a power most of us can only dream of.

PITFALLS FOR TAKERS

Because Takers tend to live at a level of financial Insufficiency, this instability can lead to negative emotional reactivity. Their interactions with others can be irrational and emotional in a way that's not helpful. The tendency to fly off the handle, emotionally, is always there. The phrases "Take a moment to get yourself together" and "Take a breath" are something Takers often hear, and it's good advice. In the same way that saving money gives you margin, financially, taking time to count to ten before having an emotional reaction gives one margin in the currency of **time.**

The danger for many Takers is to engage in risky behaviors like gambling. After all, Takers love excitement. Drinking and drugs are also temptations for Takers, but for the opposite reason. This is how a Taker self-medicates. Being such emotionally reactive people, Takers frequently have a need to calm down, and substances help with that … for a while. Then, they can often make the situation worse.

If Takers aren't nurtured and their intuitive natures aren't understood by others, their tendency to shoot from the hip can go south. Unhappy Takers create chaos by acting out without thinking. Financially, Takers often panic when things don't go as expected. Instead of taking it easy and taking their friends along for the ride, they might literally take (as in steal) from others, selfishly. If forced to intellectualize their decisions, Takers can become frustrated and show the worst sides of their Natures. If forced to follow proscribed routines and fit into uncomfortable molds, Takers are unlikely to thrive.

Takers aren't the type to think ahead, but in order to avoid the pitfalls often caused by band-aid solutions, Takers need to cultivate the ability to look ahead and choose solutions that will work in the long run, not just for now. When your happiness lies in risk and excitement, it's clear that life offers plenty of ways for those thrills to go wrong. The key for Takers'

TAKER

success is to keep a clear head in order to cultivate that naturally instinctive, intuitive nature that, when clear headed, is such a valuable and rare resource. A great exercise for Takers is to pinpoint the moment of emotional reactivity. If something sets Takers off, they can practice stopping long enough to identify what that thing was and try to figure out why it caused such an emotional reaction. Little techniques like that can help Takers bridge the gap between wild, uncontrolled reactivity and the kind of reactivity that is used at the right time, in the right way, to access a rare and powerful instinct.

DISTORTION FIELDS

When Takers aren't being their pure, instinctive selves, they crash against the Spender nature on the right side and the Giver nature on the left. Highly instinctive, Takers can also be very empathetic. It means their instincts can lead them to a high level of generosity and desire to help others. When they do this, they're trending left, toward the Giver nature. The only problem with this is that because Takers tend to live at an Insufficient Financial Level, they are often not in a position to help others. (You'll learn more about the Financial Levels in chapter six.) That creates problems both for the Takers and the people they're trying to help. On the other hand, a Taker adopting the characteristics of a deeply-feeling Spender can be very useful. When they gain awareness of their feelings, this helps already empathetic Takers enhance their fun-loving nature, thus bringing their instinctive decisions to the conscious mind.

TAKER

Taker   CHARACTERISTICS CHART

Superpowers	*Great instincts, quick reaction time, action-oriented problem solvers, highly motivated, naturally tough survivors*
Weaknesses	*Chaotic, explosive, acting/speaking without thinking, bad time management, bad at multitasking, tendency toward substance use/abuse*
Keywords	*Primal, instinctive, reactive, chaotic, resourceful, motivated, survivor, resilient, impulsive, spontaneous, playful, needy, getting, taking, anger*
Paired With	*React Financial State, Insufficient Financial Level, first chakra. (These pairings are explained in chapters 6 and 7)*
Left Distortion Field	*A tendency toward generosity, leadership, and helping others, but often without the resources to do so.*
Right Distortion Field	*Takers adopt an empathetic role and make decisions with more conscious awareness of their feelings.*

TAKER

TAKERS YOU'VE HEARD OF
The Taker as a Superhero

There are a number of superheroes known to morph, when triggered, from normal people into rageful, dissociative personalities that look like monsters and go on out-of-control, violent sprees of destruction. They are heroic when those sprees manage to destroy evil actors and preserve good ones, but one never knows quite what will happen when such a creature emerges. That hulking-beast version of the self is the ultimate Taker.

He runs entirely on emotion as if it were fuel and isn't exactly famous for stopping and thinking things through. The strength this superhero gains from his emotional nature literally saves lives sometimes, but it puts him in danger, too. What calms down that raging beast? What always brings him back to his old, reasonable self? Love, that's what. Positive emotional input.

Takers in History

ALBERT EINSTEIN

Perhaps the best-known scientist of all time, Albert Einstein's accomplishments include: providing empirical evidence for the atomic theory, determining the size of atoms, solving the riddle of the photoelectric effect, proposing both the special and general theories of relativity, predicting the equivalence of mass and energy with the equation $E=mc^2$ … and the list goes on. All over the world, this German-born physicist's name has become synonymous with intelligence, yet he is quoted extensively on the fact that intuition was the key to his genius.

Said Einstein: "The greatest scientists are artists as well." He backed up this assertion with more detail when he told interviewers that his insights didn't come from logic or mathematics but intuition and inspiration. Einstein has been quoted as saying,

> *"When I examine myself and my methods of thought, I come close to the conclusion that the gift of imagination has meant more to me than any talent for absorbing absolute knowledge … All great*

TAKER

achievements of science must start from intuitive knowledge. I believe in intuition and inspiration … At times I feel certain I am right while not knowing the reason."

For Einstein, the only difference between art and science was the choice of how to express it. Said Einstein:

"If what is seen and experienced is portrayed in the language of logic, then it is science. If it is communicated through forms whose constructions are not accessible to the conscious mind but are recognized intuitively, then it is art."

At a Kyoto physics conference in 1922, Einstein revealed the fact that he used images to solve problems and only found words or mathematical symbols for the resulting revelations later, in a secondary translation step of the process. In 1959, he told fellow scientist Max Wertheimer that he never thought in logical symbols or mathematical equations but in images, feelings, and even musical architectures. Furthermore, Einstein's autobiographical notes reveal:

"I have no doubt that our thinking goes on for the most part without the use of symbols, and, furthermore, largely unconsciously."

Einstein is famous for having said that for creative work in science, "Imagination is more important than knowledge." Einstein is the ultimate embodiment of a successful Taker—someone driven by intuition and pure feeling, who then finds ways to turn the conclusions gained from such exploration into words or other symbols that can be understood by others.

Takers in the Bible

TAKER

In the Bible, the apostle Peter had a Taker's personality. Peter was known as a pillar of the church and lauded for his enthusiasm in spreading the Word. At the same time, Peter was also known for being impulsive and brash.

This trait helped him in the sense that he trusted his intuitive knowing that Jesus was someone special and didn't hesitate to spread the word without reservation. At the same time, he was optimistic to the point of naiveté. In fact, when Jesus got out of a boat in the famous passage where he walks on water, Peter famously got out too, right behind Jesus, but of course he sank to the bottom. He didn't have Jesus' special abilities and just didn't think this through.

When it came to Peter, Jesus had to keep him in line by always taming his impulsiveness. For instance, Peter is famous for slicing off a soldier's ear when he was enraged by Jesus being arrested in the garden of Gethsemane. In another scene, on Easter morning, when John and Peter approached Jesus' empty tomb, Peter rushed in, saw Jesus' absence and ran away terrified, as opposed to John, who kept a clear head.

Using his leadership skills, Jesus took advantage of Peter's impulsive nature and gift of gab to guide him to become a great preacher. Eventually, from his pulpit, Peter brought great crowds of people to Christ because his Taker energy was channeled into the area where it was most effective.

TAKERS I'VE KNOWN

Jocelyn and Joyce

As a financial planner, I once worked with two women who liked to go in on business schemes together. They kept on trying to invest in different ideas, as they both loved the excitement they got from taking risks. It wasn't hard for me to see they were both Takers.

Unfortunately, their work together felt like living in a game of chutes and ladders. Just as soon as they made headway in any of their business endeavors, something would happen to bankrupt them and send them sliding right back to square one. They couldn't figure out why this kept happening. They understood that risk is an essential aspect of any business venture, but they didn't quite know how to manage that risk.

With some clients, I'd discourage this high level of risk at such a low level of business acumen, but knowing these ladies were both Takers helped

TAKER

me understand that the risk was the main attraction. The one thing they didn't want to give up was the excitement of risk taking. So I helped them by delving deeper into their emotional connection to risk. I asked what they got from their risks, and they both answered that it was exciting. Excitement is a word associated with Takers. They love the initial thrill of taking an intuitive leap.

I knew their strength was intuition, but their weakness was impulsiveness, so I needed to get them to stop and think about their risks a bit more. Impulsiveness is one thing, but in business you also have to do the math, and that's what they weren't doing with each of these risks. I had to help them slow down long enough to think through their next investment strategy. Those plans needed to anticipate the chutes-and-ladders experience so that they could move forward with a bit of financial margin and enough insurance to make sure they didn't fall back to square one at the slightest problem. In the long run, they continued to experience the fun and excitement they craved, but they also learned to use a practical reasoning process in order to avoid the pitfalls of the Taker lifestyle. They now have tools more common to the Earner Nature. In situations like this, real black and white numbers provide words that calm the mind and access rational, logical thought for solving problems.

TAKER

About Putting People into Categories

Now that I've taught you about the seven Financial Natures and the three Motivations that divide them, you've noticed that I tend to put people and their behaviors into categories in order to make sense of what might otherwise be a chaotic world. Some people, like me, look at the world this way, but there are also those who abhor categories.

I'm aware that some people feel insulted by being put into a category or type, as if this is a way of saying they aren't unique in their own right. I'm sensitive to this and want to make it clear that while my system does put people into categories—in fact, that is the essence of the system—that doesn't mean I think individuals are predictable or "all the same."

No matter who you are or what your Nature, you must admit that, as you go through life, you experience a lot of the same problems over and over, meanwhile you see friends and associates also repeatedly facing completely different sets of issues and problems. If we are to solve problems—in this case, problems having to do with personal finances—we must first comprehend why each of us has a tendency toward certain problematic patterns, then learn how to break those patterns. Putting behaviors and the reasons behind them into categories helps achieve this goal.

If you're like most people, you often find yourself asking, "Why does this problem keep happening?" This book is meant to help you understand that it's common to feel as if you're on a hamster wheel where additional effort leads you right back to the same problem. Everyone experiences it. That problem is not unique to you, but your version of that wheel is custom-made for your personal tendencies. In this book, as you've noticed, I describe those tendencies through the framework of:

> ➤ *your favorite Currencies*
> ➤ *your Financial Nature*
> ➤ *and your Motivation*

The more you know about your tendencies, the better able you will be to confront them. In short: the truth will set you free.

I was once asked "What are your three core values?"

"Truth, loyalty, and best effort," was my reply.

My friend asked, "Is there any truth to the idea that your loyalties are getting in the way of your best effort?"

Absolutely!! Hold onto these labels and words gently, but know that these patterns exist.

Summing Up Part 2: Self

In section one, PURPOSE, I described a way to identify your reason for taking any particular financial journey, in terms of which currencies you choose to value. Then, in section two, I gave a framework for understanding your SELF, or who you are, before beginning your journey through the financial wilderness. That framework includes seven Financial Natures further divided into three Motivations each. That makes for twenty-one different types of people when it comes to managing currency of any kind. For each of these Natures there are neighboring Natures, as I described in chapter four, about distortion fields. It is the hurricane-like action of distortion fields that tends to create, within each Nature, a sense of frustration and being stuck in a vicious circle.

Everything I described to you in the above two sections is a way of creating a visible breakdown of human goals and human nature, another way of understanding the SELF that is about to embark upon a financial journey. Looking at the diagrams in chapter three, which show the Financial Natures in a visual way, and pairing those with the detailed breakdowns in chapters five through eleven, we can clearly see an identity (or Nature) where every person resides and what each of their strengths and weaknesses are. So, if we are intrepid explorers in the realm of personal finance, we now have two of the most basic understandings needed for our journey: a sense of our PURPOSE and a sense of our SELF. But in order to get started on your journey, you need to choose a destination. The next tool I'm going to give you provides a MAP that describes seven Financial Levels, which are a graduated series of destinations. (Told you there were a lot of sevens in this book!)

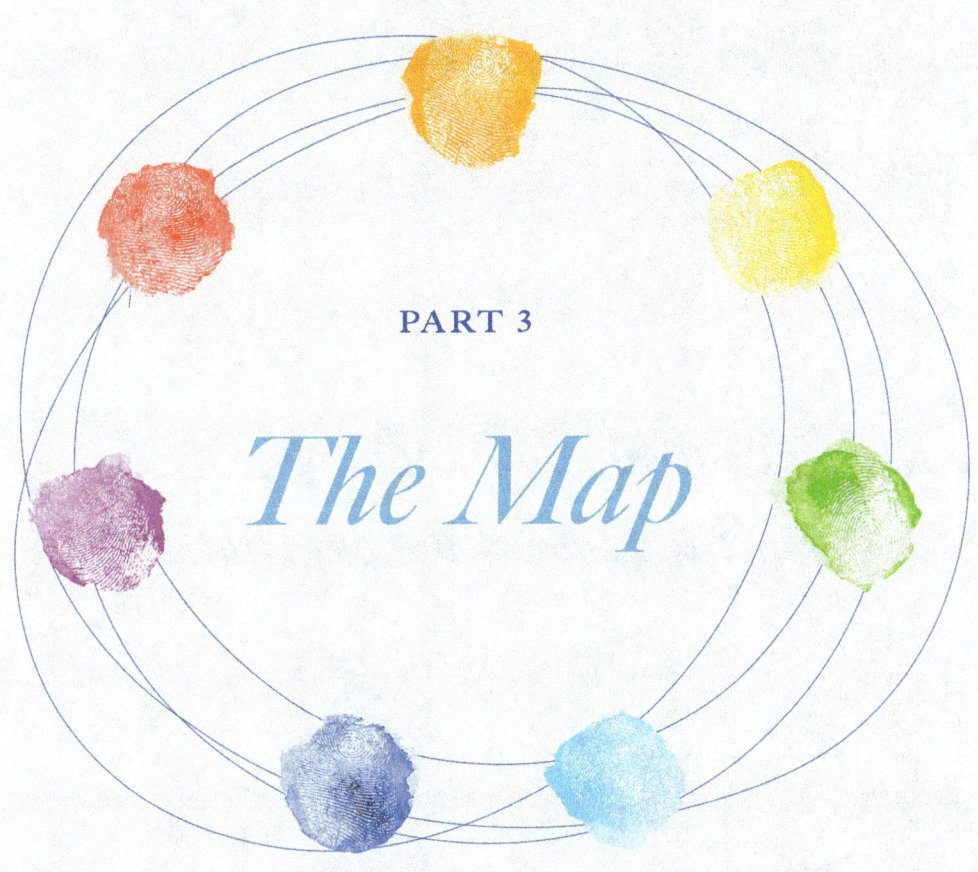

PART 3

The Map

*I speak, that you may learn
hereafter never to rest in duties*

THOMAS SHEPARD 1642

The Seven
Financial Levels

THE SEVEN FINANCIAL Levels provide a way to see the possible places you can go on this fantastic financial journey. If you think of our wheel of Financial Natures and Motivations (figure 5, page 35) as a map, it represents where you are now, so, next, we're going to add an outer ring, called the Financial Levels, that shows your potential destinations and the waypoints that will get you there.

I hope understanding the many Levels you can achieve fills you with a sense of potential and excitement. In the diagram that follows, I have added those Financial Levels, which I'll explain in detail, below.

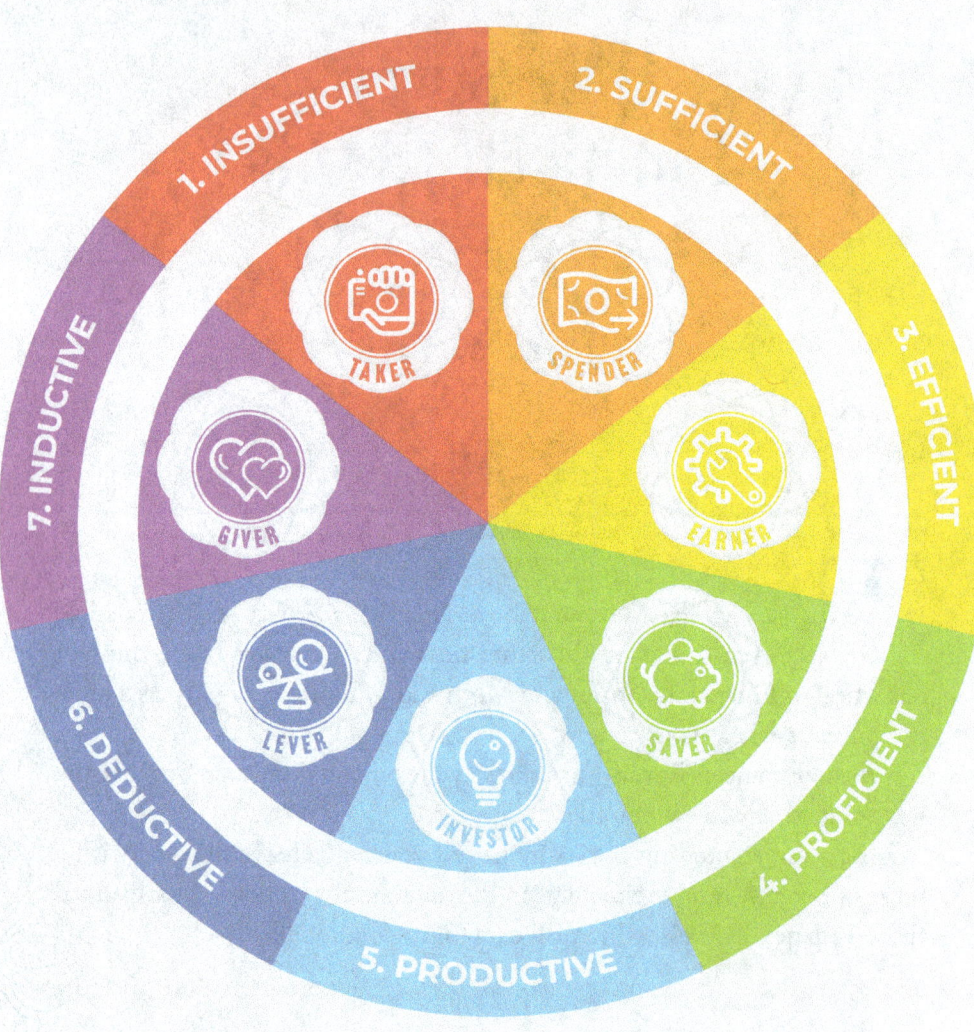

FIGURE 6

Level 1: Insufficient

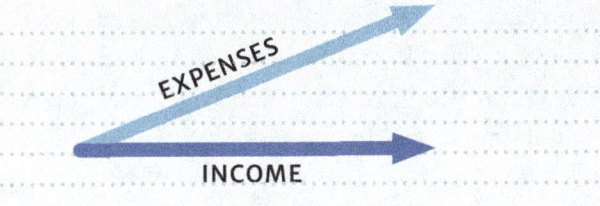

FIGURE 7

When your expenses are greater than your income, you're living in a level I call Insufficient. In fact, the whole world calls that insufficient, because it simply is. If you're living in a situation debt accumulates faster than you can pay it off, or where you are unable to pay your basic bills due to a lack of funds, you surely hope for a better future.

Few people are satisfied living in an Insufficient way. It can cause a great deal of stress, especially in any type of partnership. For some, Insufficiency means going to bed hungry, whereas for those with access to credit, worry builds as the debt accumulates beyond anything you can imagine being able to pay off. Bills sit in a pile while you wonder how you'll keep the lights on. This is Insufficiency. But there is another side to Insufficiency, too.

Insufficiency is also a time of great transition. If you can figure out how to work through this level, then it becomes a crucial part of your growth as a person. Every new endeavor begins with Insufficiency. Learning to play an instrument begins with a lot of work to do and not a lot of skill with which to do it. Raising your first child begins with a phase of complete confusion and insecurity in an Insufficient situation that seems like a constant emergency. If you like to learn new things and take risks, you're probably more comfortable with Insufficiency than others, because each time you take on something new, you have to push through Insufficiency to get to a level of Sufficiency. You're used to it.

Like in the above examples, Insufficiency can occur in any currency. People with plenty of money might start new businesses in unfamiliar fields and then find themselves right back in Insufficiency. Perhaps the entrepreneur lacks knowledge, connections, or the energy to take on the challenge. Or, of course, it could simply be a matter of Insufficient funds. Such is the fate of any entrepreneur.

If you like challenges, you get used to Insufficiency and ride the wave. But some people get stuck in Insufficiency, and it feels as if they've fallen into a deep hole. They spend years and years trying and failing to find a way out of that hole. If you're nodding yes, don't worry, this book is designed to help you.

Alice

A single mother living on government assistance, Alice was a Taker who reacted spontaneously to all her financial problems. What's more, she felt a lot of them weren't her own fault and debtors were being cruel by demanding payment when she lived under such trying circumstances. In fact, she couldn't even talk about money without flying into a rage.

Alice had maxed-out her credit cards and also owed a lot of money to friends and family, who had grown resentful of these debts. Thus, her lack of money (**stuff** currency) was causing a deficit in **relationship** currency, too. Instead of working with Alice on the mathematics of her debt, I approached the real problem—the emotional one. In this case, a lack of trust (**relationship** currency) was at the root of the problem, and it was only getting worse. The more she refused to acknowledge her debts, the less people trusted her.

I told Alice the only way to end her financial nightmare was to swallow her pride and admit she was in a mess of her own making. She had to stop blaming the world, sit down with her debtors, and humbly offer them payment plans she could afford to honor. Facing the truth like this can feel frustrating, even humiliating, for Takers, who hate to measure or plan any aspect of their lives, but people admire those who face their fears. Doing so would earn her great admiration from her debtors, who could see what a big step this was.

Level 2: Sufficient

FIGURE 8

Those in a Sufficient level have enough to cover their expenses in the long run, but not necessarily day-by-day. Should an emergency arise, there are often no funds to cover it. Should you desire anything above the basics of life, tough luck. There just aren't extra funds for fun. Another trait of those in Sufficiency is a tendency to bounce up and down between having a little extra and not having enough. If you spend money on something fun this month, you'll be broke next month and have to find a way to cut back. Once you're at an even keel again, you'll repeat the same behavior. Zigzagging up and down from surplus to deficit is the only way you get to have anything extra, if you're living in Sufficiency.

When it comes to the different currencies, Sufficiency can also mean just barely having enough **time** to take care of your needs. You fall down exhausted at the end of the day, having fulfilled your requirements but without a single, spare minute. If you do take a vacation, it is typically followed by months of catch-up work. Sufficiency in your **relationships** means you're part of a community that, generally speaking, supports you. It doesn't exactly lift you up. It doesn't extend credit to you. It doesn't make you feel like the world is your oyster, but your **relationships** help you keep your head above water, and that's the main thing.

Sufficiency feels wonderful to those emerging from Insufficiency. For them, just being able to break even every month is a big win! People can live their entire lives in a state of economic Sufficiency and be perfectly happy as long as their **health**, **relationship**, and **time** currencies are also Sufficient. But if ill-health or any other emergency occurs, that's going to send you diving back down into Insufficiency, and it'll be an unpleasant struggle to get back up to break-even.

Level 3: Efficient

**INCOME / EXPENSES
ALIGNED**

FIGURE 9

People in a level of financial Efficiency cover their expenses on a regular basis. The stress caused by fluctuating in and out of debt is gone. You live paycheck to paycheck without accumulating debt because your income exactly matches your expenses. Any fluctuation in income or expenses can still cause stress, but typically you don't have to worry from day to day about meeting your needs. You have stability without room for luxuries. You're not visibly moving up the socioeconomic ladder, but you're comfortable and you're making it.

Some people in Efficiency have worked so hard to get there, they think they're at the top of the financial pyramid. Being financially stable is a great feeling for those who have suffered from financial Insufficiency and Sufficiency, but the state of Efficiency doesn't leave a lot of room for additional education, retirement planning, big dreams, or leaving a legacy. It's a decent place to live, but you can rise higher!

Level 4: Proficient

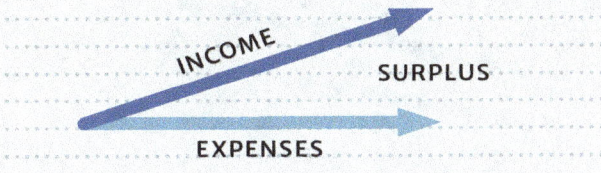

FIGURE 10

If you have achieved Proficiency, that means your income covers your expenses and leaves some surplus. That's right, you now have retirement savings, back-up savings, and all the security that goes with having that little extra to ensure your long-term happiness.

If you are Proficient, you keep your surplus in a basic checking account or other financial vehicle that doesn't use your money particularly wisely but simply saves it. You may be the sort of person who enjoys having money in the bank so much that you like to look at the numbers add up every month. Or perhaps you just don't know enough about financial instruments to be able to make that surplus money pay off for you. You've got it, though. Even if it's being saved inside your mattress, you've got that surplus that eliminates the sense of panic often felt by those at Insufficient and Sufficient Financial levels, and you've risen above the point of breaking even. Saving your surplus as an emergency fund is also called "operating with margin."

Level 5: Productive

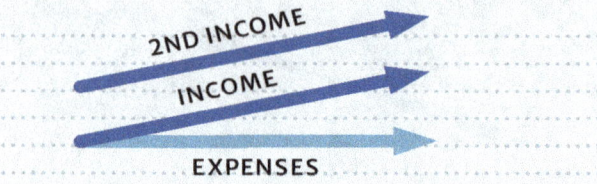

FIGURE 11

Beyond Proficiency, we get into three phases where you're able to generate more money without more work. The first is the Productive level. That surplus income you generated in the Proficient level is now invested in such a way that it produces a second income. One common example is the interest you receive from keeping money in a long-term savings account. In this way your money is working for you, instead of the other way around.

Exactly how and where to invest your surplus income is, of course, a matter for a financial planner or other knowledgeable professional to determine, but the fact that you have educated yourself about investment options is the key to achieving the Productive level. Some invest in financial products while others invest in real estate, art, or business ventures. Either way, Productive people turn that surplus income into dividend-producing assets that function as a secondary income.

Level 6: Deductive

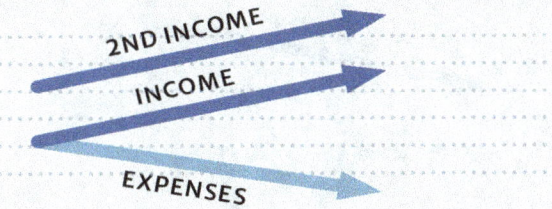

FIGURE 12

Now that you've gone through the stage of being Productive, you've got investments producing a second income for you. That's nice, isn't it? It feels like free money, but it's just the spoils of all the hard work you did to get to this place. The Deductive level prompts you to ask: What should I do with that second income? If you set up some of your bills to be automatically paid out of the account generating the second income, it will reduce the bills you have to pay out of your primary income. In the graph above, you can see how this widens the gap between expenses and income. An endowment fund is an example of a deductive strategy.

Level 7: Inductive

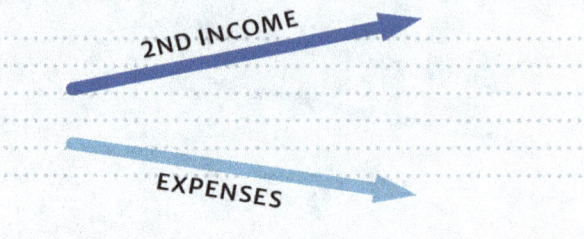

FIGURE 13

Finally, at the Inductive level of your financial life, that second income being generated by your savings is covering all of your expenses. You don't actually need to work anymore, so if you choose to continue to work for income, that's now "fun money." You're living off the dividends from your investments. While achieving this stage is a dream for many people, it can also be a let-down, because when some people stop working, they get bored. Now that you no longer have to engage in the day-to-day hustle and bustle of income generation, you might wonder what to do with yourself!

This level is like retirement but also like a rebirth. Those in the Inductive level sometimes decide to entertain themselves with something new and different like starting a new business, traveling the world, learning an art form, or getting in great shape. Each of these endeavors is a risk and an adventure and causes a plunge right back into Insufficiency in one or more of the four currencies.

Having worked hard to ascend to the peak of Inductivity, it might seem counter-intuitive to go right back to being Insufficient, but this time you'll be Insufficient in a whole new way. You'll have the money to support yourself, so the Insufficient phase will feel like learning, exploring, risking ... in short, a new adventure!

Roger

My client Roger was a successful businessman and a Lever. By a stroke of luck, his company went public, its stock price shot up, and Roger became a multi-millionaire overnight. He was now at Financial Level 7, the Inductive Level, where he could live solely off the secondary income from his investments. So, he retired, but Roger and his wife Celia felt disoriented by their newfound wealth. Roger's work was a big part of his identity, and Celia's life as a housewife had changed, too, as she could now hire help. They both felt superfluous. This is a common phenomenon: When people rise to the Inductive Level (7), financially, they often drop to the Insufficient Level (1), emotionally.

I suggested the two of them try a real estate venture to give them a new direction in life. Roger and Celia went through a lot of emotional upheaval as they adjusted to this second career. As they worked to lift themselves out of emotional Insufficiency, it felt nice … but strange. In the long run, they were successful up to Level 6. They could have taken their real estate business all the way to Level 7 but chose not to, as they preferred their new, easygoing lifestyles, which were highly emotionally fulfilling. Their decision to put the brakes on their successful second careers is a great example of the fact that there is no obligation to work toward Financial Level 7. Like Roger and Celia, we must all weigh financial solvency against the lifestyles we prefer and set our goals appropriately.

What Holds People Back

I think everyone would agree that ascending to higher Financial Levels is beneficial. Whether you seek security for yourself or funds for a charity, you can always think of something worthwhile to spend money on. But there is a psychological component that hinders the journey up the financial ladder. A lot of people get stuck along the way because they can't mentally adjust to moving up. After all, moving up means moving on, and it may mean you don't get to work directly with your friends anymore or live in the same place. To avoid change, many people sabotage themselves. I personally encountered an excellent example of this when I worked with a well-known weight-loss program. I was reminded of that work recently when I happened to talk to my neighbor Jim, who noted that my recent weight loss showed. I told him I had lost thirty lbs. and was so glad, but I noted that I could no longer wear a lot of my favorite clothes.

"Yeah," said Jim. "That's the problem. I'm so cheap, if I lost weight, I'd just put it back on again so I wouldn't have to buy new clothes."

It might sound strange, but I had similar conversations with many members of the weight-loss group. Some folks, especially those with a Protector motivation style, were so dedicated to preserving the status quo and so conservative about engaging in new spending that they literally sabotaged their own efforts to improve. In this weight-loss program, such people shied away from buying the new clothes and enjoying the new lifestyle that came with weight loss. Consciously they wanted to become healthy, but subconsciously they feared change. This is just one way people sabotage their upward mobility—in this case, in the currency of health.

When people join a weight-loss program like this one, they experience positive results by tracking their caloric intake, and they get positive reinforcement by making new friends who are doing it too. When such people succeed in losing weight, the health problem goes away, but a financial problem emerges: the need for an investment in new clothes. A relationship problem also emerges: They have made friends in the weight-loss support group and don't want to leave.

While they may not consciously realize it, the prospect of graduating from the weight-loss group means the loss of their enjoyable meetings. So, instead of keeping the weight off, as they originally planned, group members tend to lose five lbs., then put it back on, then lose ten lbs., then put that back on, then lose fifteen, but put it back on again, and so forth. As long as their weight continues to fluctuate, they're engaging in the program—so they can stay in the support group—but they haven't succeeded, so they'll never be forced to graduate from the group.

Back in the early 2000's, the program gained an understanding of this dichotomy, so they changed their model. In the new model, they used individual coaches instead of group meetings. But in so doing, they sacrificed the social aspect of the program model and lost a lot of clients. To get the clients back, the program revived the original support program but also created a second "encouragement" group into which successful dieters could graduate. Now, instead of just giving dieters one goal, they provide a scaffolding to take them from one goal to the next and to the next, with support along the way.

Their improved system is how my financial planning model works, as well. Those who love change and growth will enjoy seeing themselves traveling the paths I have described. Those who simply abhor change will be reassured by the fact that with each new Level they achieve, they continue to have guidance into the next Financial Level. This isn't a one-time-and-done system for getting out of a financial hole but one designed to support you in going as high as you wish to go, knowing what steps to take along the way.

Everything Flows
Nothing stands still

HERACLITUS

The Map of
Financial Levels

1. INSUFFICIENT
2. SUFFICIENT
3. EFFICIENT
4. PROFICIENT
5. PRODUCTIVE
6. DEDUCTIVE
7. INDUCTIVE

TAKER — PROTECT · MANAGE · PURSUE
SPENDER — PROTECT · MANAGE · PURSUE
EARNER — PROTECT · MANAGE · PURSUE
SAVER — PROTECT · MANAGE · PURSUE
INVESTOR — PROTECT · MANAGE · PURSUE
LEVER — PROTECT · MANAGE · PURSUE
GIVER — PROTECT · MANAGE · PURSUE

FIGURE 14

Y ou may notice in this diagram that each Financial Level is paired (by color coding) with one of the Natures. This is because each Nature has a tendency to live at one of these Financial Levels. For instance, a Taker is likely to live his life at a level of Insufficiency. That doesn't mean he's doomed to stay there, and it also isn't necessarily a bad thing. Remember that Insufficiency isn't just a matter of not having enough money, it can also be a wonderfully transitional time of learning and evolving into something new.

A Taker needs to learn how to cycle through these Financial Levels so that each time he returns to Insufficiency, it is with a new type of deficit, a new goal, a new currency that he wishes to build. In Part Four, I'm going to teach you how to start that cycling process, but for now, just remember that in order to have a dynamic, engaged life in all four currencies, it's important to learn to cycle through the seven Financial Levels, in order, always building your skills, your security, and your investments in all the currencies that matter to you.

This book is not designed to teach you how to "get rich," as if attaining wealth were a static thing. Instead, it's designed to teach you how to find what you value and keep on getting richer and richer in **stuff**, valuable experiences, meaningful **relationships**, memories of **time** well spent, and new discoveries that always keep you growing. With that in mind, this wheel diagram isn't static, either. The inner ring (the Financial Natures) rotates clockwise, like so:

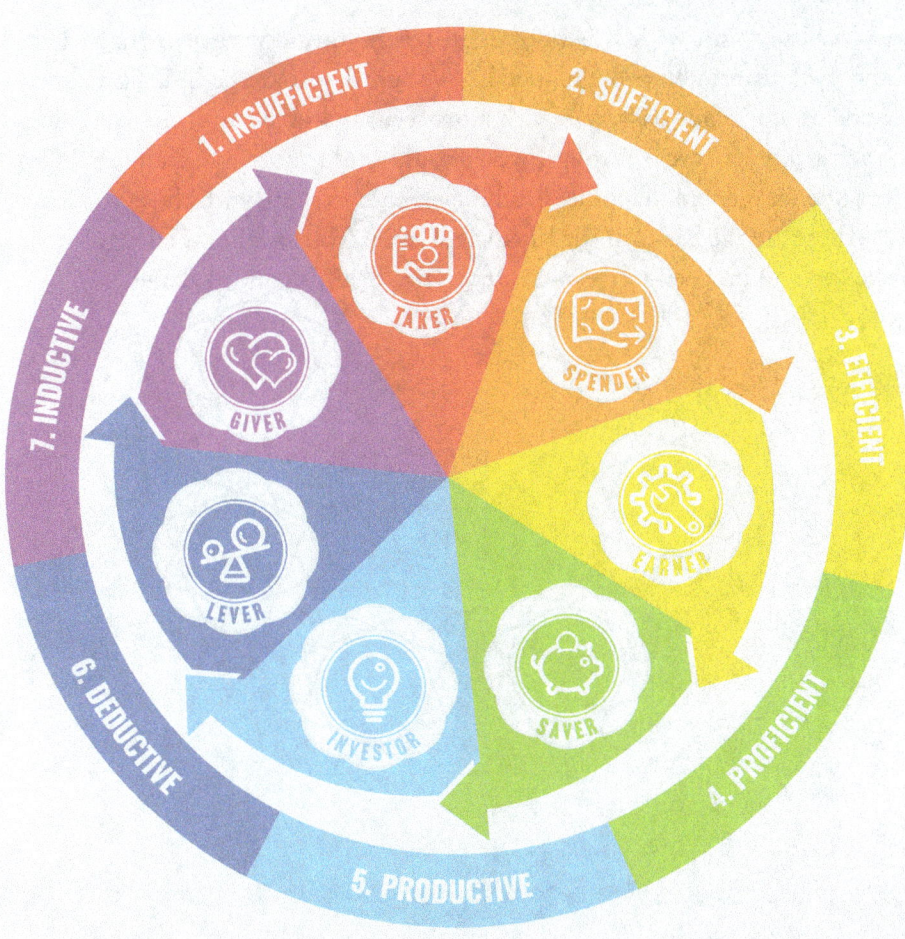

FIGURE 15

Remember that the Financial Levels are the destinations and waypoints on the MAP of your financial life. The object of the entire game of financial planning is to refrain from remaining static but instead, rotate the central wheel clockwise so that you experience each of these Financial Levels in order. Whether you live in the place of a Taker/Manager, an Earner/Protector, an Investor/Pursuer, or any other spot on the wheel, you can see by the color coding exactly what Financial Level you are likely to consider "home," and therefore which Level will be next for you.

My intention with this book is to teach you how to turn that wheel and cycle through each Financial Level until you are right back to your color-coded "home base," but with more security in the currencies you value. Each time you cycle through, you should build more and more savings, confidence, general happiness, and have more to share with those you love.

Those are the basics of the Financial Levels. You now know enough about the topic to proceed to the next step: what I call Financial States.

Summing Up Part 3: The Map

In Part One, you learned to identify a PURPOSE for your financial journey by taking a look at the currencies you value. Then, in Part Two, you learned more about your SELF by finding your unique Financial Nature and Motivation. In Part Three, above, I introduced you to a MAP of your financial journey describing the potential destinations in order. Now that you know the different Financial Levels available, you understand that you can't just jump from a state of Insufficiency to that of Inductivity in one big, magical leap. No matter how fast or slow you take the financial journey, and no matter which Financial Level you strive for, you must achieve each Financial Level in turn, thinking of each one as a waypoint toward your chosen goal. But the question remains: what is the technique by which you (your SELF) can achieve your unique PURPOSE by navigating this financial MAP?

To move toward your goal, you'll need a tool. Just as one lost in the forest can use a COMPASS to find one's way, the next section of this book provides an intellectual tool that functions as that COMPASS. The tool is called the Financial States. Some might prefer to think of them as "energetic states," so if that makes sense for you, feel free to do so. This COMPASS adds another wheel to the circular diagram I introduced above in figure 15, and it's the key to making this whole system work. You've waited long enough! Here we go…

*Have fun, its later
than you think!*

WALTER "GRAMPS" SHEPARD

PART 4

The Compass

Allow yourself to think only those thoughts that match your principles and can bear the bright light of day. Day by day, your choices, your thoughts, your actions fashion the person you become. Your integrity determines your destiny

HERACLITUS

The Seven Financial States

I CALL THE NEXT part of the system "the COMPASS" because, like a real-life compass, it is the instrument you use to navigate toward your destination. Rest assured, the thing I call the COMPASS isn't some big stock tip or secret Wall Street maneuver. Instead, it's an understanding of what I call the seven Financial States, which are ways of being and behaving in your financial world. Some of these States will feel comfortable and familiar to you, while others definitely will not. In order to move up and improve yourself, though, don't you always have to step out of your comfort zone?

The seven Financial States enable you to accomplish something new that will, eventually, take you back to the state where you are most comfortable, only at a higher level of currency. They are closely tied to the seven Financial Natures, yet unlike the Natures, they are not fixed, or assigned at birth. These States can be consciously adopted by any individual. The key to moving forward in any currency lies in making the decision to take on behavior that makes you embody a new Financial State. You could also think of this as a decision to resonate at a new "energetic frequency." For instance, the Taker Nature tends to live at a Financial State called *react*.

The Seven Chakras and the Seven Financial States

One of the most ancient and well-known "sevens" is the set of seven chakras, or energy centers within the human body. My wheel of Financial States is a somewhat similar series of energetic places designed to keep your financial life in balance. With both the chakras and the Financial States, the idea is not to find the "best" one and remain stagnant there, but to always have a sense of moving through them in order as you progress through life.

In Yogic thinking, the blockage of a chakra's energy can cause physical and emotional disorders, whereas the "balancing" of these chakras leads to health and happiness. Similarly, figure 2, page 27 in chapter three illustrates what it's like when we get stuck in one of our Financial States and can't seem to move forward.

The Taker Nature contains a lot of qualities, like having good instincts and a quick reaction time. Takers seize opportunities and are highly motivated, resilient, and tough, and their instincts make them excellent at survival. All those things are true, but the Financial State associated with the Taker is the state of *reactivity*. This is the very essence and most salient aspect of any Taker's financial personality.

In the same way that our diagram shows Takers tend toward a state of Insufficiency, I'm adding a color-coded wheel to the diagram (between the outer wheel showing Financial States and the inner wheel showing Financial Natures) that shows Takers tend to live in a Financial State called *react*. The color coding in figure 16 shows you each Financial Nature, what Financial Level that Nature tends to consider "home," and which Financial State tends to also feel like "home" to that Nature.

From the diagram, you can see that a Spender's most salient Financial State is *feel*. So, while Spenders tend to be confident, high-energy people that are fun, exciting, and dramatic, they are primarily characterized by an ability to be empathic with others—an advanced ability to feel.

Looking at the Earner, you'll notice this person's Financial Nature aligns with *think*. Earners are hard-working, determined, resolute, and engaged. Efficiency and competence are paramount in this personality, which is excellent at allocating resources, managing time, and taking bold action. In order to achieve all that, Earners have immediate access to intellectual reason for the sake of problem solving. The Financial State of any Earner is *think*.

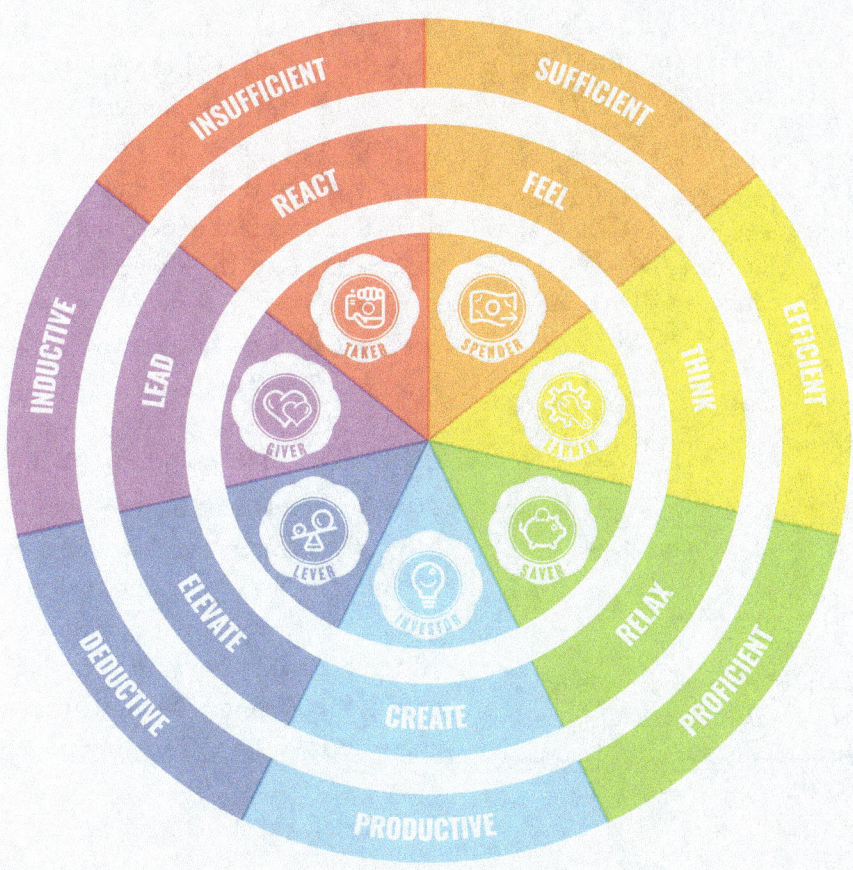

FIGURE 16

Savers are perpetually prepared, steadfast, and independent. They are characterized by composure, frugality, and a sense of caution. Therefore, their Financial State is that of *relaxation* into a comfortable life. Having taken all precautions against undue risk, Savers exist in a state called *relax*.

Creativity and innovation are the province of Investors. This Financial Nature tends toward intelligence, charm, and a high-achieving attitude. Always attempting to multiply the value they have access to, Investors will use any resource in order to do that. As such, these are the celebrators of

The **Root Chakra** is located at the base of the spine. When balanced, it feels confident, independent, and strong. When out of balance, it causes purposelessness, instability, insecurity, and fear.

The **Sacral Chakra** is located in the lower abdomen and contributes to vibrancy, positivity, compassion, and intuition. Imbalanced, though, it causes irritability, sexual dysfunction, and a lack of creativity.

The **Solar Plexus Chakra** is located at the solar plexus and provides confident, productive, focused energy. When imbalanced, it causes digestive problems, diabetes, depression, anger, and perfectionism.

The **Heart Chakra**, located near the heart, contributes to feelings of compassion, optimism, and friendliness. But if imbalanced, it causes mistrust, anxiety, jealousy, and moodiness.

creativity, and their Financial State is called *create*.

The Lever Financial Nature is one that always seeks to invent systems to make life easier. Levers will take on any difficult task, but rather than toil away to complete it, they'll spend their **time** building a machine or designing a system to accomplish the task more easily. In this sense, Levers *elevate* themselves and others above the mundane work-a-day world. Their Financial State is called *elevate*.

The Giver is a Financial Nature tending toward generosity, leadership, teaching, and making the world a better place. Givers are visionaries who lift others up by celebrating their best qualities and expressing gratitude for all the gifts they have, in turn, been given. The Financial State that most characterizes the Giver is *leadership*. They *lead*.

In brief, the Financial States, in order, are:

➤ *React*

➤ *Feel*

➤ *Think*

➤ *Relax*

➤ *Create*

➤ *Elevate*

➤ *Lead*

These States are represented in the wheel format because there is no beginning or end to them. Once you get to *react*, you'll eventually return to *feel* and start the cycle again. Each of us begins this journey at a unique location. Typically, you will begin at the Financial State paired with your Financial Nature, as can be seen in figure 16 on page 139, but whatever State you happen to be in right now is also fine. The important thing is to recognize which Financial State is next and push forward at a pace that's right for you, in order to avoid stagnation.

How to Use this Information

In your financial adventure, once you have identified the currencies you'd like to focus on (your PURPOSE), you then need to understand your SELF (your Financial Nature and Motivation) before beginning the journey toward your next goal on the MAP provided by the Financial Levels. The list of seven Financial States given above, in a specific order, is your tool, or your COMPASS that will help you move from your current Financial Level to the next one. We can revisit the process visually in the diagrams below.

First, you take the Financial Natures Assessment at the link on page 22 of this book or the number of the figure 1 to identify which Nature on the wheel belongs to you. Then, assess which of the three Motivations you have, seen in figure 14.

The Throat Chakra, located at the base of the throat, brings on creativity, self-expression, and good communication. Blocked, however, it causes timidity and bad communication.

The Third Eye Chakra, located between the eyebrows, is responsible for intelligence, intuition, and self-knowledge. A lack of balance here can cause headaches, blurry vision, and eye strain.

The Crown Chakra, located at the crown of the head, is the center of spirituality and enlightenment, allowing for the flow of wisdom and cosmic consciousness. Imbalanced, however, it can cause self-destructive feelings.

The outer wheel of our diagram provides the MAP that enables you to select your current location as well as a desired destination and the waypoints you'll need to pass along the way. As a financial planner, I do this by gathering information about your income/expenses and assets/liabilities.

Now that you understand the different Financial Levels, you'll want to next identify at which Level you are in your chosen currency, right now. It may or may not be the Level typically paired with your Financial Nature. If you have a movable model of this wheel at home, go ahead and pair up your Financial Nature with your current Financial Level. The colors may or may not match up.

When you insert the middle wheel describing the Financial States and look at the full, color-coded diagram, you'll want to assess at which Financial State you feel you currently exist. If you have been feeling like a hamster on an endless wheel of toil, there's a good chance your Nature and your State are matching colors, but not necessarily. Essentially, if you're stuck in your financial life, you need to identify at which Level and at which State you are stuck.

Then again, if your Financial Nature is aligned with its color-coded Financial State and Level, it can also mean you're comfortably resting where you belong in preparation for your next adventure in currency acquisition. Only you can assess your level of comfort and decide if you're feeling stuck/stagnant or perfectly comfortable.

The key to following through on any plan or adventure is learning how to rotate these wheels in order to advance. Think of the wheel of Financial States being like the minute hand on a clock and the wheel of Financial Levels like the hour hand. You must go all the way around the wheel of Financial States in order to facilitate the wheel of Financial Levels moving just one notch.

These groovy diagrams are fun to look at, but of course if you want to improve your finances, you need to see how others have moved from one to the next Financial State and Level. That's what I'm going to discuss next. I'll use a story to explain how Freddie FreeSpirit, the fictional character you met in chapter four, achieved his life's goals by moving from *react* to *feel* and so on along the wheel of Financial States.

Freddy Navigates the Financial States

L ET'S REMEMBER GOOD old Freddie FreeSpirit, whom I used above, in chapter four, to illustrate the idea of distortion fields. Freddie is a Taker, whose primary way of being is to *react* impulsively. He captures life and drinks it in, always taking his time, taking pleasure in every moment, and taking it easy. Takers like Freddie intellectualize life less and excel at things that require great instincts like music, art, and athletics. Freddie never plans or manages any of the currencies in his life: the ultimate devil-may-care type of person.

A surfer dedicated to the lifestyle, Freddie lives with roommates in a bungalow near the beach, works at a surf shop, and hangs out the rest of the time, so how in the world is Freddie ever going to achieve anything in life? First, we have to find out what currencies he values and therefore what he wants. It might not show, but Freddie really does have goals. In fact, he'd like to become a pro surfer and travel to the great surf spots on the globe.

Just like most of us, Freddie feels like he's taking action toward his goal every day but always seems to fall short. Traveling the world costs money,

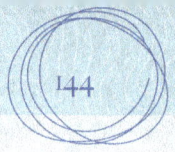

and try as he might, he can't seem to save enough for a bus ticket to the next town over, much less a flight to Oahu's Banzai Pipeline.

We have identified Freddie's Nature: Taker. His Financial Level is Insufficient, so that's where he resides on the financial MAP. Now is the time to apply our COMPASS, a.k.a. the intellectual tool called the Financial States, to help Freddie make his dreams come true.

Like all of us, Freddie's Financial Nature has a tendency toward distortion, or what feels like running but getting nowhere. Being a Taker, his Nature is to *react* to things without stopping to think or even analyze his feelings. That said, Freddie will never improve his financial life unless he learns to stop instantly *reacting* and instead pause to analyze his feelings before taking action. *Feel* is the next financial state on the rotating wheel, so Freddie needs to learn to slow down long enough to actually feel and understand his feelings before acting on them.

> *History is a child building a sand-castle by the sea, and that child is the whole majesty of man's power in the world*
>
> HERACLITUS

When Freddie is operating in his distortion field, he comes close to registering and acknowledging his feelings, but the whirlwind sweeps him from the brink of *feeling*, around the reactivity at the core of his nature, to the Financial State on the other side of *react*, which is *lead*. There is a part of Freddie that longs to lead others, but he can't manifest the strength needed for that until he moves forward through *feel*, then *think*, *relax*, *create*, and *elevate* until finally he has built up the inner resources to *lead*. So when he tries to go straight from his *reactor* nature to a position of leadership, he tends to fail.

All Freddie needs to do in order to escape this repeating cycle is *feel*, meaning confront his feelings about money. If he can stop beating himself up for his naturally *reactive* state of being and simply accept that he has a lot of feelings about money and the difficulty of its acquisition, this is a great start. The first step to any change, after all, is seeing the problem clearly and accepting that it exists.

In this phase, Freddy hasn't come up with a solution, yet he is preparing himself, emotionally, to do so. Accepting his emotions, breathing through them, and acknowledging them fully will enable him to see the potential for action with a positive outcome. This acceptance will build his confidence and help him progress from paralysis to action and from a vague sense of need to one of goal-focused desire.

Once Freddy confronts his feelings, he turns the notch on the wheel of Financial States from *react* to *feel*. His Financial Level, however, is still at home in Insufficiency.

Next, Freddie must come up with some kind of plan that will help him overcome his emotional reticence about financial growth. This requires him to *think*, which is the next Financial State. Since *think* is the natural province of the Earner, Freddie must take on the practical qualities of this Financial Nature just long enough to reason through the steps required to become a pro surfer.

Most likely, his emotions about attempting to become a pro surfer include the fear of failure, something that's very common to anyone considering an ambitious move. But having confronted the existence of these emotions, he resolves to take action anyway. In the *think* phase, Freddie identifies a schedule of surf competitions that, if he enters and wins, could attract the sponsorship that would get him the funding he needs.

The danger for those who habitually reside in the *think* State (Earners) is that of thinking about something so much that it leads to paralysis and paranoia. Hypochondriacs, for instance, think about their health so much that they can manifest health problems just by worrying them into existence. So, while thinking is important for problem solving, it is also important to keep moving to the State of *relax*.

Typical of the frugal Saver, *relax* is a State between that of coming up with a plan and that of taking action, which enables people to get used to the plan, become familiar with its specifics, and ease into the idea of making this big change. For Freddie, *relaxing* is crucial so that he doesn't get intimidated by the big plan he has made and end up backing out. Having moved into the *relax* state, Freddie can turn the wheel of Financial States one more notch.

Finally, Freddie *creates* a calendar of events. In this phase, he enters the competitions and buys the necessary equipment, plane tickets, and so forth. This is the moment of creativity, the moment of building something new. His plan is afoot!

When time for his first surf competition arrives, Freddie embodies the state typical to Levers: he *elevates*. He gets on that surfboard and carves those waves the way only he knows how. He uses his incredible talent to *elevate* the crowd's appreciation of his magnificent sport. In so doing, he hopes to have leveraged (or traded) what he has (talent) for what he needs (money and opportunity). In competition after competition, he shows them what he's got. In so doing, Freddie turns the wheel of Financial States one more notch.

Once Freddie achieves the plan he created back in the *think* State, he truly ascends to a new level in terms of his personal achievement and confidence. No longer is he a "good-for-nothing surf bum." Now—win or lose—he's a serious athletic competitor who has taken the action needed to move his life up a level. At this point, Freddie hopes he has made an impression and will be approached by sponsors. If he gets that sponsorship, Freddie will advance to the *lead* Financial State.

Now that he has achieved something truly great, he sees himself as a leader, someone who can get the job done. No longer is he an ordinary beach bum. He may use this leadership position to advise his friends as to how he achieved and how they may be able to do the same. If he gets financial sponsorship, he might *lead* by giving something back to those who helped him out when he was down. Or Freddie may simply *lead* himself into the next phase of achievement. Having gone through the full wheel of Financial States, Freddy now sees he has also moved up in the Financial Levels, from Insufficient to Sufficient.

Next, Freddy will return to his familiar *react* phase, where he celebrates the victory! Then he'll prepare to go through the wheel of Financial States again in order to get to a higher level of competition. As long as Freddie keeps using the tool of Financial States, going through each phase in order, the sky is the limit for his ability to achieve.

In this scenario, Freddie started off at Financial Insufficiency, but with the sponsorship money, he is no longer living in debt. The money isn't much yet, but he has finally achieved Sufficiency, where his income and his debts are matched. Once he goes around the wheel of Financial States again, and wins more competitions, he may get the chance to advance to the next Financial Level and the next. There is no obligation to do so, of course. Freddie can stop financially achieving at whatever level is comfortable for him.

But things don't always go our way, do they? What if sponsors don't approach Freddy after his stunning performance? As the old adage says: "If at first you don't succeed, try try again." There is no reason to give up, but Freddie will certainly *react* differently. This time, he may not complete the cycle and move into the leadership phase but instead, *react* with disappointment, which is also a valid emotion. Life is full of disappointments, but when we see our reactions to them as just steps along the path, hope is there.

Once Freddie has picked himself up again, in order to continue moving through the wheel of Financial States, he'll just have to recognize his feelings of disappointment, then, when he's ready, move forward to the *think* phase again. As such, he'll want to ask himself what he might do differently in the next competition or how he might better approach sponsors. Before taking action on those ideas, he'll want to *relax* and really think it through. Perhaps his *creative* stage involves creating a list of surfwear companies and a list of questions, such as, "If they didn't choose him, why not? Did his surfing lack skill? Showmanship? A certain difficulty level?"

When he progresses again to the State of *elevate*, this time he leverages his social skills and boyish good looks to get meetings with those higher-ups and ask those questions. In so doing, he lets the sponsors know he is ambitious and actively interested in going pro, thus *elevating* his personal brand.

It's scary to get out there in front of people and announce your ambition, but hey, if it was easy, everyone would do it. Right? Having introduced himself to the sponsors in question, Freddie will probably have to go through another round of competitions, but this time he has a bit of a leg up. He isn't unknown. There is no telling how many times Freddie will have to try to achieve his goal, but with an understanding of the Financial States and their order, Freddie has a tool he can use to keep on making plans and making progress.

Ideally, Freddie will keep on trying, keep on cycling through the Financial States until he is able to move up one Financial Level at a time. It's important to keep in mind that the value of certain currencies isn't static. At one point in life, Freddie may think of **relationships** as the only currency that matters, but if he has a family one day, he might become more focused on **stuff**. Then again, being an athlete, maybe the ongoing **health** of his loved ones and himself remains the paramount goal for Freddie throughout his life. The point is, moving up a Financial Level might mean making more money, but then again, it might not. If money isn't what you want, there's no need to think of progress in terms of **stuff**. Individuals all have their own PURPOSE, which naturally changes throughout the various phases of life.

In an ideal world, Freddie will become so successful that he goes through a phase of really embodying the visionary, future-oriented, *lead* Financial State, which prompts him to serve others with the wisdom he has gained along the way. Maybe he even becomes a mentor for youngsters, teaching them to shoot for the stars.

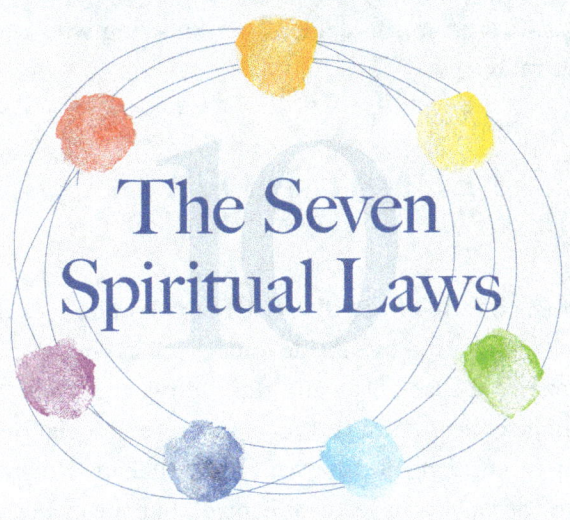

The Seven Spiritual Laws

I HAVE PERSONALLY BEEN deeply influenced by Deepak Chopra's Seven Spiritual Laws of Success, and the parallels I find between the seven Financial States and these spiritual laws is striking. With full recognition of Chopra's intellectual ownership of the Seven Spiritual Laws, I'd like to discuss these briefly here and show that relationship.

1: *The Law of Pure Potentiality*

AND ITS RELATIONSHIP TO THE
FINANCIAL STATE: React

Chopra designates the "Law of Pure Potentiality" as the first law of spiritual success. This tells us we, as beings, are pure consciousness. That means within each of us exist all possibilities and infinite creativity. It is up to us to access the aspects of our Natures that most interest each of us, which is our SELF. Our potentiality is the source of all intelligence and power.

Says Chopra, "Success in life depends on knowing who we really are." I couldn't agree more.

EXTERNAL MOTIVATORS TO THE SELF

In discussing the nature of the SELF, Chopra emphasizes that the ego is an aspect of self influenced by outside forces such as circumstances, people's opinions, power or the lack of it, and the approval of others. Our egos live in fear of failing to please others. Our egos create a social mask that helps us fit into society, ensuring our survival. More than anything, our egos seek the approval of others and a sense of control, but the externally motivated ego is not the pure SELF.

INTERNAL MOTIVATORS TO THE SELF

The pure self is in harmony with nature. In fact, because the pure self contains infinite potential, it has the ability to form a bond between our desires and the power that makes those desires manifest. We access our pure potentiality through tuning out external influences and simply being in our real nature. Pure potentiality isn't about acting or feeling but about being. That's right: pure potentiality is about your *reactive*, intutitive nature, which is connected to pure universal consciousness. Ways to access this side of ourselves include stillness and meditation, including the active practice of nonjudgement.

Wisdom is the oneness of mind that guides and permeates all things

HERACLITUS

Judging things as right or wrong interferes with your ability to simply know things as they are. A surfer doesn't judge a wave as good or bad but simply reacts to the swell and flow of it in order to be one with it. A tree doesn't judge the plants around it as good or bad but simply finds ways to share resources and build the ecosystem together. One way to access pure potentiality is to spend time in nature—the ultimate place of nonjudgment and constant flow. When tuned in to the nonjudgmental law of Pure Potentiality, we feel ourselves to be beings of pure consciousness and harmony, even in a world filled with chaos.

REACTORS (TAKERS) EMBODY THE LAW OF PURE POTENTIALITY

This attitude toward life is the gift provided by those in the Financial State called *react*. Typically, Takers tend to live in this state, but anyone striving to move through the Financial States in order to improve their Financial Level will spend some time here, intuitively reacting to their circumstances.

Takers aren't always the most successful, organized, or efficient people in the room, but as far as being tuned in to the natural flow of the world, the essence of nonjudgmental listening, they're experts. So with this first law, Chopra encourages everyone to make this aspect of life part of their daily experience. That means spending time in silence, nonjudgment, and communing with nature. By the same token, I describe the *reactive* Nature (typical of the Taker) as the first in a

The Financial States of Love

When we talk about relationship currency, we're talking about love in its various manifestations. But love plays different roles in our lives. As such, when we evaluate the status of our relationships it's important not to fall for the misconception that romantic love supersedes all other types. Stable relationship currency should include a balance of all the types of love necessary to emotional and social health. The ancient Greeks grasped this concept very well and gave us words to describe the many types of love in our lives.

Interestingly, the Greek words for love correspond to the seven different Financial States and also come into play when we talk about our Motivations, so just as Spenders (for instance) tend to feel most at home in the feel Financial State and the Sufficient Financial Level, they're also likely to have a specific type of love that is prominent in their lives. Let's take a deeper dive into the many types of love that exist in our emotional landscape.

Philautia and Miseo

PHILAUTIA is self-love, a pre-requisite for being able to love others. I think of those Financial Natures motivated to Protect as being profoundly influenced by philautia, which enables one to give love freely to others. Without Philautia, one can fall into self-obsession and the overwhelming need for external validation, which leads to an excess of another type of love: miseo, a state of non-love or dislike.

People you don't like are those for whom you feel miseo. MISEO is also a word for a love/hate relationship. This sometimes-conflicted type of love can deeply influence the struggle to increase our relationship currency, but it also tempers us with wisdom. Sometimes you just know certain people are not good to be around. Feeling and acting on the natural aversion that comes from miseo protects you from their influence.

series of energetic States that guide us toward successful acquisition of our chosen currency. Takers surely make great use of Chopra's first law, the Law of Pure Potentiality.

2: The Law of Giving and Receiving

AND ITS RELATIONSHIP TO THE FINANCIAL STATE: Feel

Chopra's second spiritual law of success is The Law of Giving and Receiving. This law takes into account the reality that the world is a place of dynamic exchange. You already know that people come and go from your home, and cars come and go on the interstate. So, by extension, the world is a place where giving and receiving are part of the natural flow of energy. If we want to keep the flow happening, we must participate in both sides of the flow of life energy. There must be giving as well as receiving in our lives—in whatever currency works for us at the time.

People typically engage in the economy due to their feelings. When we feel flush, we give and spend. When we feel desperate, we take and save. Feelings direct us to take risks sometimes and act conservatively other times. Overall, Chopra makes the point that one must give and receive with honest, joyful purpose, not grudgingly. It is the intention behind the giving and receiving, the feeling behind it that keeps your spiritual currency flowing.

The Law of Giving and Receiving deals with money more acutely than any other of Chopra's seven laws, and in discussing it, he emphasizes what I also firmly believe: money is a symbol of life energy. While this book presents a practical, grounded system for managing currency, Chopra's book taps into how your behavior is likely to affect the positive or negative influences that come your way. His ideas can't be proven; they're spiritual in nature. My system is much more practical and doesn't require any particular type of faith or belief in a higher power. That said, I can demonstrate how Chopra's spiritual Law of Giving and Receiving manifests within the system this book presents.

HOW GIVING AND RECEIVING WORK, IN A SPIRITUAL CONTEXT

Chopra's spiritual law states that stopping money's circulation (hoarding) means that no more currency will come to you because none is being given by you. One must not be afraid to spend, just as one must not be afraid to accept currency that is given or earned. Keeping currency flowing through the channels of giving and receiving is key to a strong personal (and world) economy. But don't worry, there are a lot of ways to participate in the economy other than giving away your hard-earned cash.

Sometimes we feel at rock bottom, as if we have nothing left to give. And yet, with all the currencies at our disposal, there is always some way we can contribute to others. Perhaps you can pass on some wisdom to a youngster, help a friend move a couch, or load an elderly person's groceries into her

Philia and Storge

PHILIA is a term for a deep soul connection between loving partners. Philia can come into play within platonic or romantic love where two partners have shared values, trust, and a spiritual connection. I pair philia with the Financial State *relax*. Savers, who prefer to be in a *relaxed* State, are most likely to have plenty of pure philia energy in their lives.

The Greek term STORGE, a variation of philia, describes the caring love between members of a family, keeping in mind that such love expression is seldom equal. For instance, a parent is likely to be more of a love giver, while a child is more of a love receiver, due to their different needs. I think of this need-based exchange of love as relevant to Earners, who are often in a State of *think*, where selfishness drops away and one is able to look at what's best for the overall situation.

Pragma, Agape, and Meraki

PRAGMA is a type of love based upon a sense of duty or shared goals. It overlaps with the family love found in storge but can also be found in professional environments. It requires one to uplift a community rather than oneself. As such, pragma is associated with the elevating state common to Levers, but any Nature motivated to Manage also understands the pragmatic nature of pragma.

AGAPE (also called thelema) means unconditional love that leads to altruistic behavior beyond one's duty and toward the betterment of society. It is found in those with the Financial Nature Giver. Whenever we share our expertise and talents with the larger world, expecting nothing in return, we experience agape.

Greeks thought of the creative act of making, building, or inventing as an expression of love called MERAKI. Because true creativity requires wholehearted commitment to one's craft, its expression is an act of love whose object can be uncertain. Some creators do so to honor God or their parents, but often, the reason people feel compelled to create is mysterious, even to the artists themselves. Investors, who thrive in the Financial State create are most likely to experience meraki on a regular basis.drops away and one is able to look at what's best for the overall situation.

car. Little gifts like this mean a lot, and they keep the currencies flowing. The key, though, is to always give joyfully, unconditionally, and from the heart. I don't mean to imply this is always easy to do.

When we're worried about one or more of the major currencies in our lives, it can feel very hard to give anything, even our attention, to any entity outside of our personal problems. The tendency to hoard what you have at points like this is natural. We've all felt that way. But Chopra's spiritual law reminds us that we exist not in a vacuum but within a universal economy. He says the best way to get more of anything is to engage in the world of commerce where that currency is involved. Chopra suggests that when we freely and enthusiastically give any type of energy, the world gives back to us in the same currency.

If you want love, he suggests that acting with truly felt loving kindness to those around you will get you more of the love you seek. If you want affluence, enthusiastically helping others become more affluent will result in you becoming more-so. That doesn't mean you should give away all your money and expect a plane to drop a box full of dollar bills in your front yard. Rather, you might share the wisdom in this book and others you may have read. Or you could help a job seeker make a connection with a potential hirer. Perhaps you know a young person ready to take on his first job and can advise him on the wisdom of saving 10% of his earnings. All of these are ways to contribute to the affluence of others. Spiritually, Chopra insists that sharing what you have of this energy will come back to you in the form of money. As for me, I can't comment with authority on the spiritual side of things, but I can give you an assessment of giving and receiving from a financial planner's standpoint.

HOW GIVING AND RECEIVING WORK IN A FINANCIAL CONTEXT

We all exist in an economy. For those who need money, the tendency for Savers and Earners is to save what you have while trying to figure out how to get more. But staying in this place can result in stagnation. Meanwhile, Investors and Levers might invest what they have in "get rich quick" schemes or gambling enterprises and hope to double their money that way—a risky endeavor. Givers, Takers, and Spenders are a bit more tuned in to the need for active, ongoing commerce, but even they can get stuck in a rut if they only participate in their favorite part of the economy.

Eros, Ludus, and Mania

EROS is the Greek term for beauty, sexual desire, and lust. When healthy, eros seldom stands alone but is paired with something more emotionally fulfilling, like philia. Takers, who often find themselves in the feel Financial State, are likely to be most prone to feeling an abundance of Eros.

LUDUS is the very essence of carefree playfulness. Happy children enjoy ludus! Yet, when highly sensual, it can be paired with eros to create the kind of relationship that makes you feel "in love." Along with eros, ludus is associated with Takers or anyone in the feel Financial State.

MANIA occurs when any love becomes obsessive, jealous, possessive, and an unhealthy fixation. All Natures are prone to take their favorite type of love too far and fall into mania, which is why we want to cycle through the Financial States rather than get stuck in one for too long. Mania is most common among those Motivated to Pursue, as they're prone to excess and extremes.

Type of love	Quick description	Direction: Internal or external	Corresponding Financial State, if any	Corresponding Motivation, if any
Philautia	Self love, self confidence	Internal: self		Protect
Miseo	Non-love or love/hate relationship Against	Internal: self-protection	Provides a sense of caution and self-protection to all States	
Philia	Deep soul connection. Platonic love.	External: the other	relax	
Storge	selfless love paired with duty, usually between family members	External: the other	think	
Pragma	Duty or shared goals	External: family, culture, community	elevate	Manage
Agape	Selfless, altruistic love	External: the larger world	lead	
Meraki	Love of creating	Internal: one's own inspiration	create	
Eros	Beauty or Sensual love	External: a lover or object of beauty	feel	
Ludus	Playful love	External: a friend	react	
Mania	Obsessive love	External: an object of fascination		Pursue

Spending, earning, saving, investing, leveraging, giving, and taking are all ways to participate in the economy—as long as you cycle through all of these and don't just get stuck in one. This brings us back to the importance of learning to consciously direct yourself to cycle through the Financial States so that you don't get mired in hoarding, impulse buying, being a recipient of charity, gambling, borrowing, or giving money away for any extended period of time. All are important parts of a working economy, and no single one is "the key." These facts about how personal and world economies work back up Chopra's spiritual belief in the Law of Giving and Receiving.

3: The Law of Karma, or Cause and Effect

AND ITS RELATIONSHIP TO THE FINANCIAL STATE: Think

Karma is a concept misunderstood by many, but Chopra defines it quite simply as the fact that every action has a reaction. He says that when you apply conscious thought to your actions (instead of just reacting by habit) you can bring about better results. Better "causes" result in better "effects." In other words, "you reap what you sow" … so think before you sow. The Law of Giving and Receiving is certainly similar in that it suggests if you lovingly give in a certain currency, that currency will come back to you tenfold—a karmic reaction. But the Law of Cause and Effect takes this idea into a new realm. This law is intent upon having you think through your actions, no matter what they may be, before you do anything.

> *Those who love wisdom must investigate many things*
>
> **HERACLITUS**

For instance, arguments tend to start when one person either purposely or inad-vertently insults another. Without thinking, the other person *reacts* to show his or her offense, then tries to even the score by insulting the first person back. The first person doesn't consider the score even at all, and reacts again, creating a potentially endless series of "score settling." The Law of Cause and Effect suggests that this entire kerfuffle could be eliminated at the beginning by the recipient of the initial insult making a thought-out, conscious (instead of instinctive) choice to refrain from being offended at all. Chopra's Law of Cause and Effect suggests this change in behavior is not only possible but necessary for your success as a happiness-seeking human. This behavior change is also the topic addressed by my system's description of the *think* Financial State.

MAKING THE SWITCH FROM REACTING/FEELING TO THINKING THINGS THROUGH

Often, we act in ways that we feel are out of our control when this is not the case. We are conditioned to *react* in certain ways, the way Pavlov's dogs

All are one.

HERACLITUS

were conditioned to salivate when they heard the sound of a bell. Just like those dogs, most people are conditioned to *react* well to compliments and badly to insults, thinking these are the only *reactive* possibilities, but they are actually conditioned

responses. When we stop both *reacting* by instinct and behaving according to our *feelings*, we can think:

> ➤ *What choice am I about to make?*

> ➤ *What results do I want from it?*

> ➤ *What will be the consequences of this choice, and are they in line with the results I seek?*[1]

Many people feel it isn't possible to be that rational when under pressure or in a strong emotional state, but it certainly is, when you make the conscious choice to do so. Of course, having gone through the states of *react* and *feel* first help you prepare for this transition into the state of *think*. That's why these Financial States are in the particular order they're in.

In a state of *react*, someone might respond to an insult with a sharp word or punch in the nose. In the state of *feel*, the same person will be aware of his hurt feelings and perhaps respond with an honest expression of those feelings. But when in the state of *think*, the same person will hear the insult and consider:

---

1 One tool that can help you think about your feelings
HTTPS://FEELINGSWHEEL.COM/

> ➤ *Did that person mean those words the way I understood them?*

> ➤ *Do I need to take this insult personally or can I just chalk it up to the other person's lack of sophistication or education?*

> ➤ *If given a chance to take back the insult, might this person feel sorry for having said that?*

> ➤ *Can I learn anything from this person's opposite point of view?*

Every highly emotional person knows that developing the ability to think things through is a big help in any sort of conflict situation. At the same time, those naturally oriented toward logic and away from emotion eventually learn that *reacting* and *feeling* have important roles to play in the pursuit of happiness and currency, too. The Law of Karma, or Cause and Effect, reinforces my own belief in the fact that rationally thinking things through is an integral part of the cycle of Financial States.

4: *The Law of Least Effort*

AND ITS RELATIONSHIP TO THE FINANCIAL STATE: Relax

The Law of Least Effort encompasses something called the "principle of defenselessness." The idea is to give up on recruiting people over to your point of view. It suggests that by doing less and observing more, you'll achieve your goals in a way that's harmonious with the world—in short, you'll set yourself up for a win-win solution. After all, in nature, grass blades don't try to behave like sunflowers, racoons don't try to behave like bears, and mountains have no shame for casting their shadows over valleys. Everything behaves according to its intrinsic nature, without trying to be something it isn't.

According to the Law of Least Effort, seeking power or control over others (trying to change the world, in other words) goes against the harmony of nature. By the same principle, acting for only personal gain or chasing an illusion of happiness thwarts nature. "Least Effort" means that one can open oneself up to the happiness that already exists in the moment rather than go elsewhere in search of ego-based dreams.

YOU CAN LOVE YOUR LIFE WHILE ALSO STRIVING TO IMPROVE IT

Chopra's fourth spiritual law reflects the Financial State *relax*. Once individuals have spent time being *reactive*, then consciously *feeling* their feelings, they then graduate to the *think* phase, where they consider their goals and make plans. At this point, before taking action, before asserting one's will over the world, it's a good idea to enter the *relax* phase. Here, you nonjudgmentally observe the situation, the plans you've made, and the things that are and are not within your control. This relaxation, or state of effortless existence, helps you understand the difference between making plans to change your life situation and being attached to how you wish things were. You can simultaneously love your life and strive to improve it. Both are possible, and that is the message of both the Law of Least Effort and the Financial Nature called *relax*. After all, problems are simply the seeds of opportunity.

The Law of Least Effort and the Financial State called *relax* both reflect the idea of non-attachment to one's situation, surroundings, possessions, and status. True relaxation and effortlessness requires total acceptance of the present moment, especially if that moment is one on the cusp of transition. Rather than living in the future (where you will have solved your current problems) or the past (where you had no solution for them) you now relax into the present. Here, the future is unknowable, so happiness must be found right now, despite all the transitions you anticipate.

5: *The Law of Intention and Desire*

AND ITS RELATIONSHIP TO THE FINANCIAL STATE: Create

The Law of Attention and Desire states that real power is found when desire is fueled by conscious intention, which is to say a person has a desire and takes action to achieve it, but does not live in a state of attachment to the outcome of that action. Most people think of desire for anything as being intrinsically tied to getting the outcome one desires. But in this way of thinking, we view it differently. Here, we focus our intent upon the future. We're not neutral. We definitely have an intent. However, the key to success is to not live in the illusion of that future. Our attention remains in the present even though our desire is projected into the future.

After all, the only thing that is truly real is the present moment. The future is a fantasy, and the past is a memory. One cannot travel into the past, nor can we experience the future, because as soon as we're there, it's the present. There is no point in projecting our desires into the past, as that can never be changed. Doing so would be neurotic behavior. But we can project our desire into the future, and doing so yields results. Thus, intention in the present moment paired with desire projected into the future is a creative force to be reckoned with.

ATTENTION AND INTENTION EQUAL CREATIVITY

This law makes use of two crucial concepts in Chopra's system of spiritual laws: "attention" and "intention." Our attention energizes matter in order for our intention to transform it. These are also the forces inherent in the Financial State called *create*. Should my success rely upon my ability to build a better mousetrap, I'll have to put my attention on that project. Whatever I take my attention away from will wither and die, according to the principle of attention.

If, previous to this, I was designing a time machine made out of a DeLorean, the fact that I've now switched my attention to the building of the better mousetrap will cause the previous project to collect dust. By the same token, if the world puts its collective attention upon the industrialization of its cities and the production of luxury items using fossil fuels, it diverts its attention away from spiritual growth and the protection of nature. In recent decades, we have seen the results of this attention shift, haven't we? Thus, attention determines where creativity will manifest and where it won't.

Intention is the force that triggers the transformation of energy. With my attention on the project of building a better mousetrap, I'll then weld steel rods together, concoct tempting assortments of cheeses for bait, and construct clever new structures for trapping mice. Intention is the creative force that transforms things that are at the center of our attention. For this reason, Chopra's Law of Attention and Desire correlates with the Financial State of *create*.

6: *The Law of Detachment*

AND ITS RELATIONSHIP TO THE
FINANCIAL STATE: Elevate

The Law of Detachment takes the Law of Intention and Desire to a new level. In law five, we established that focusing on an intention manifests a creative force, but being attached to the outcome of that creativity drags you down. For this reason, remaining detached from the outcome of your efforts is crucial. Put another way, detachment means knowing you are powerful and capable, that whatever outcome arrives, you can make the most of it. Chopra describes detachment as "unquestioning belief in the power of self," so it is tied to self confidence.

When we cycle through the Financial States and arrive at elevate, we're at a place where we seek to collaborate in order to lift up our communities.

We create more ease in life by leveraging one asset against another to achieve big-picture goals, even if we have to take on short-term debt. In other words, we no longer focus on the contents of our own wallets but rather the **health** and wellness of our family, company, town, or country over the long term. Levers, the Financial Nature most prone to being in a state of elevate, must experience a certain detachment from life's daily ups and downs in order to comprehend this big-picture, long-term financial plan. Those who remain attached will be so busy obsessing about their needs in the moment that they won't see the wisdom of borrowing money to leverage it for a long-term profit. Detachment lets you see the big picture of life.

SELF CONFIDENCE IS KEY TO DETACHMENT

The idea of detachment and belief in the power of self circles us back to law one, the Law of Pure Potentiality, which states that knowing thyself is key to understanding all of your potential. When it comes to the Law of Detachment, that self-knowledge produces the confidence you need to detach from the outcome of your work. After all, we work with a view to a certain outcome, a sense of "how things should be" at the end of our efforts. If we didn't, we'd be spinning in circles, but life always seems to teach us that working toward something requires you to also have a sense of humor about it. How often do things turn out "just the way you planned?" Hardly ever! Yet, most people still expect outcomes to be predictable and get upset when they aren't. Doesn't it make more sense to set your plans and put in the effort while also remembering that the world just isn't that predictable? This is the essence of the Law of Detachment. Those who elevate, or seek enlightenment, must integrate this "letting go" process into their quests.

No matter what type of greater force you believe in—from simple scientific principles to any of the world's conceptions of God—there is always a reminder that the world's "big picture" is greater than your selfish needs. Trust in the wisdom of that big picture is the key to the principle of detachment. A lack of trust in the rhythms of nature, the universe, God, or whatever you want to call it results in a belief that "if it is to be, it is up to me." In this mindset, you think nothing positive can manifest unless you force it into existence. The result is a lot of hard work, and guess what ... things never turn out exactly as you expect, anyway. For Levers and others who seek to elevate, such hard work is anathema. At this stage, we want to achieve success easily and effortlessly by leveraging our existing surplus (rather than working hard) to get the assets we require.

DETACHMENT IS ABOUT LOOKING AT THE BIG PICTURE

In addition to making life harder, the "If it is to be, it is up to me" mindset causes us to attach to symbols of success such as bank accounts, homes, cars, and possessions. But this is a type of insecurity. Because such things are transitory and illusory, they tend to produce anxiety—an emptiness within. The fear of losing these symbols creates a sense of rigidity within that prevents us from enjoying the natural ebb and flow of currencies such as **energy**, **time**, **relationships**, and **stuff**.

Have fun, its later than you think!

WALTER "GRAMPS" SHEPARD

Instead, the Law of Detachment encourages us to accept and embrace the unknown at all times, remaining in a state of alert preparedness. This way were're open to solutions that appear, rather than trying to force our own solutions upon the world. Working from this place of detachment means trusting that your ego is not the only force that determines positive outcomes. This puts us more in harmony with whatever big-picture success we seek. The "universe," after all, is harmonious. In the small-picture view of things, life can seem random and chaotic, but in the big picture, it all makes sense.

7: *The Law of Dharma or Purpose in Life*

AND ITS RELATIONSHIP TO THE FINANCIAL STATE: Give

With his Law of Dharma or Purpose in Life, Chopra perfectly expresses the leading nature of the Giver. This law tells us that through spiritual awareness we can become cognizant of the special talents we have to share with the world. And with this knowledge, we determine our purpose in "the big picture" of life on Earth. Being able to spend our lives exulting in our own unique brand of service to the world provides an unparalleled sense of purpose—a deeper reason for living than mere ego-fulfillment.

Those who go through the *lead* Financial State rise to a level where they realize their work and goals have not all been to serve themselves but in order to realize a higher purpose. Importantly, one doesn't have to be a millionaire or an enlightened monk to enter the Financial State of *lead*. It is merely the next step after *elevate* (where we work to uplift the community) and before *take* (where we accept that sometimes we need to be on the receiving end of things). One can lead and serve in many ways as we cycle through the Financial States to achieve our currency of choice.

PURPOSE IS AN EASTER EGG WORTH THE HUNT

Finding purpose in life isn't a one-and-done exercise but something we go through repeatedly with a view to developing and enhancing it. All students who have changed their majors and all artists who have changed their mediums can tell you that purpose is a tricky thing to find. Discovering the unique talent you have to share with the world is a lifelong process for most of us but a worthwhile endeavor. Yet, it isn't the outcome of our leadership (or gift to the world) that makes it all worthwhile. It is actually the search for that unique gift or purpose itself that guides us to a sense of inner fulfillment. This is because with each element of the search we gain a little bit of enlightenment, a little hit of that essential sense of purpose. This provides the steady drip of fulfillment that gets us through the dark times.

While we may go through life consciously thinking we're seeking money or love or status, the underlying bedrock of what we seek is purpose. There isn't a person on Earth who hasn't at one point asked themselves: "Why am I here?" We know we must ask this of ourselves, because in the answer to this question lies true and lasting abundance.

THE CONNECTION BETWEEN DHARMA AND ABUNDANCE

The term dharma literally means "to uphold," although it is generally thought of as a word describing our purpose on Earth. Knowing our purpose is how we uphold others and how the world upholds us. Those who fulfill their true purpose on Earth see through the illusion of society's conditioning and ask, "What is a higher cause than the trappings of a good life?" It is true that finding true purpose brings about a state of spiritual fulfilment, but with this comes something more tangible: lifelong abundance.

Money, fame, and other types of fortune are common manifestations of abundance, but they don't guarantee happiness. As we discussed earlier, the superficial trappings of fame tend to leave individuals feeling anxious and full of the fear of loss. However, the one thing nobody can take away from you is your true calling or true purpose in life. Chopra asserts that when you find this purpose, your life will automatically become abundant—kind of like "God's" or "the universe's" way of rewarding you for pursuing a worthy goal.

This is the very essence of the Financial State I call *lead*. *Leading* is the phase where you know yourself enough to freely give of yourself to the world—where you fulfil your dharma.

Summing Up Part 4: The Compass

For many of us, our lives cycle between distortion and distraction. In the meantime, techniques we have learned allow us to calm ourselves down, yet, without a compass to point the way, we still often wander in a circle. The path forward will appear when we have clarity. On a journey through the woods, we can be lost, wander, or sit and ponder, and there are times when each of these can feel like the right circumstance for our lives. We do, however, have goals and want to avoid spending our lives going in circles. For this reason, we use techniques like those in this book to achieve clearly defined, step-by-step objectives. This way, moving forward is as easy as navigating by the stars on a clear night or hiking through the wilderness on a trail that is clearly marked.

PART 5

Your
Guidebook

INDUCTIVE

DEDUCTIVE

PRODUCTIVE

PROFICIENT

EFFICIENT

SUFFICIENT

INSUFFICIENT

FIGURE 17

The Evolution Matrix

Freddie FreeSpirit's journey has made you familiar with the moving wheel diagram pictured in figure 16. This diagram is useful for guiding every Financial Nature into its next state, but I'd like now to introduce you to a 3-D diagram that shows, in another way, how someone like Freddie can see his financial situation improving. I call it the Evolution Matrix.

Here, you can see how if Freddie started down there in the *react* area of the Insufficient level, then worked his way up through *feel*, *think*, *relax*, *create*, *elevate*, and *lead*, he will have come full circle to the point where his Financial Level can rise from Insufficient to Sufficient. Yet because this diagram isn't flat, you can visually see here that the circle takes him not right back to the beginning but to a similar journey that now occurs at a higher level. When Freddie cycles through these states one more time, he will go up a level again, and so on.

This diagram illustrates how, in finances, just like in every other life-learning experience, we are always moving, never standing still. Even if you slide all the way back down to Insufficiency, you have gained something in the currency of knowledge, even if it was a lesson in what not to do.

Having seen Freddie's journey, you now have some idea as to how the tool of Financial States is similar to a COMPASS that guides you from notch to notch on the outer wheel of Financial Levels. Your knowledge of the Financial States points you in the direction of the next stop on your journey. It helps orient your map so that you don't spend time looking over your shoulder or walk backwards through life.

Depending upon your Financial Nature, you may feel at home any place on the wheel of Financial Levels, but knowing the technique I just described can help you defy the condition that is common to your Nature and rise above, always aiming to improve your life in terms of the currencies that you most value, and always returning to the Financial State and Level where you feel most comfortable.

In this example, we discussed Freddie's life in terms of his finances and career prospects, but you may seek advancement in other currencies. The same technique applies. So, let's take a look at how you can use the Evolution Matrix as another type of MAP that helps you figure out exactly where you are now in any given currency, where you'd like to be, and the path to get from here to there.

Your Currency Matrices

NOW THAT YOU have a sense of the four currencies, your own Financial Nature, the Seven Financial Levels, the function and order of the Financial States, and the three- dimensional Financial Evolution Matrix, let's bring all those elements together with an exercise and a visual aid. In making plans for improving your life in any currency, the first step is to assess where you are, currently, in that currency, by assessing your Financial Level. Then, you'll look at the possibilities and decide where you'd like to go on your journey, or what Financial Level you'd like to shoot for.

Time

When you take a look at the following grid, you'll notice that the Financial Levels are listed along the left-hand side and the Financial States lie across the bottom, in order. The purpose of this grid is to ascertain where you are in each of

Applicants for wisdom do what I have done: inquire within

HERACLITUS

the currencies right now so that you can set goals for improvement. This is not a test! There are no right answers as long as you answer truthfully for you, right now.

Mark with an ✗

	React	Feel	Think	Relax	Create	Elevate	Lead
Inductive							
Deductive							
Productive							
Proficient							
Efficient							
Sufficient							
Insufficient							

THE Y AXIS

When it comes to the currency of **time**, we're typically talking about **time** management. Ask yourself: Do you feel you have enough free **time**? Do you spend enough **time** with your loved ones, with your work, and with other things that are important to you? Are you able to dedicate **time** at will, or is all your **time** management done by others, for you?

INSUFFICIENT
If you never have enough **time** for what's important, then you're in an Insufficient state.

SUFFICIENT
If you sometimes have enough **time** for everything but not consistently, then you're in a Sufficient state.

EFFICIENT
If you have exactly as much **time** as you need for all of life's essentials, with no margin, then you exist in a state of Efficiency.

PROFICIENT

If you have a little bit of extra **time** every week, where you enjoy the luxury of deciding how you'll spend that surplus time, then congratulations, you've made it to Proficiency in the currency of **time**.

PRODUCTIVE

Productivity in the currency of **time** means you can "bank" some of your **time,** also known as enjoying "flex time." Perhaps you're free to take **time** off work to attend a family function (without having to make up that **time** at work, later). Or maybe you can take **time** away from your family to spend some relaxation **time** all alone … again, without going into "**time** debt" where you'll have to make up for the lost time, later.

DEDUCTIVE

Reaching the level of Deductivity with **time** means your "expenses" in terms of **time** are all taken care of, and you have a steady influx of free **time** that you can spend according to your own discretion.

INDUCTIVE

Finally, in Inductivity, you have no obligations at all when it comes to **time**. Not everyone wants to reach this stage, as having a schedule of important things to do tends to help many people organize and pace their lives. But if all your **time** is entirely your own and you can apportion it as you see fit, you are in Inductivity.

THE X AXIS

Disregarding, for the moment, what your essential Financial Nature happens to be, let's assess where you stand in terms of the crossroads of **time** and the Financial States. It's important to remember that the amount of time you spend in each of the Financial States can last a minute, a day, a year, or any period of time, but you have control over this. It's up to you to assess when you've achieved what you set out to achieve in each State and to consciously choose to move on in order to eventually progress to the next Financial

Level. That said, let's nonjudgmentally assess where you happen to be, right this minute, in terms of your Financial State.

REACT

When you're *reacting* to time, you're typically running directly from one activity to the next. If you have enough **time** to stop and feel stressed about it, then you have moved on to the state of *feel*, but as long as you're just doing, doing, doing, and not bothering to stop and experience your feelings, you're in a *reactive* state. Sometimes the reactive state is exactly where you want to be, like during an emergency such as a house fire, violent attack, or medical situation. These are moments where stopping to analyze your feelings would not be appropriate. Your ability to instantly react to emergencies, in real time, is invaluable.

Hopefully you're not in a *reactive* state right now, as you read this book, but I'm sure you can remember passing through this State many times in life. Those who habitually overanalyze can fail to take advantage of the intersection of the **time** currency and the *react* Financial State, whereas others can get stuck at the intersection of **time** currency and *react* State (also known as "panic mode") when it would me more appropriate to move on to *feel*, *think*, etc.

FEEL

When it comes to time, are you currently in a state of *feeling* something about it? This could be stress, but it could also be elation. Is **time** an emotional factor for you, right now?

> ➤ *Do you feel anxiety at not having enough time for the activites you value?*

> ➤ *Are you overwhelmed with joy because you just got to a place where you have much more free time than before?*

> ➤ *Are you bored and feel you have too much free time and not enough to do?*

> ➤ *Do you spend so much time at work that it's causing you a lot of stress?*

> ➤ *Are you happier than ever to be spending productive time at work?*

In any of these cases, you're *feeling* a lot of emotion around time, and you're currently in a State of *feel*.

THINK

Perhaps you're in a very logical place with your relationship with time. Do you primarily think about **time** in a non-emotional way, scheduling it carefully and apportioning it as needed? Is **time** something you can control and regulate by thinking ahead, making careful plans, and sticking to those plans? If so, you're in a state of *think* when it comes to the currency of **time**.

RELAX

If you have **time** to relax and just do nothing special, then you're in a state of *relax*. Keep in mind that relaxing is different from spending **time** playing and doing scheduled recreational activities. Relaxing is literally doing nothing scheduled, nothing accomplishment-oriented, just taking it easy. If you feel relaxed right now and also relaxed generally about the way **time** is being spent in your life, you've achieved this State.

CREATE

When in a state of *create* with money, we're investing it to create more money. When it comes to the currency of **time**, that means you can spend **time** on something that actually creates a sense of you having more time. Of course, unlike money, we all have just twenty-four hours in the day, so you can't create a stockpile of actual time, but if, for instance, you build a system that automates something that used to take a lot of your time, then you have *created* something that leaves you with more free **time** than before. That's how we create **time** (even if it's an illusion). If you are actively building a system that will create more free time, you're in a State of *create*.

ELEVATE

Spending time *elevating* means lifting up yourself and others with this currency. If you can delegate to others because you have money or position or power, then you may be able to get around to more important things. If you spend time taking care of the shopping for a busy friend or babysitting for a mom with too much to handle in a day, you're *elevating* others in the currency of time. In this case, *elevating* doesn't apply to just any type of community service, but only that which saves time for you and others.

LEAD

Being a *leader* when it comes to the currency of time usually means teaching others how to better manage their time. You might teach a student a more efficient way to memorize facts for a test or teach a parent how to use an app to have groceries automatically delivered. When you help others by doing time-consuming things for them, you're *elevating* your community, but when you teach people how to live in such a way that they manage their own time better (ultimately without the need for your help) that's the act of *leading*.

FINDING YOUR PLACE ON THE GRID: NOW, LATER, TODAY, AND TOMORROW

Going back to the grid above, you'll want to mark the square where your Financial Level in the currency of time intersects with your Financial State in the currency of time, right now. Because Financial States can change quickly, this is an assessment you can take every day, or even several times a day, to establish exactly where you are in the currency of time.

Next, you'll want to decide where you aspire to be on the grid. That's your goal on this journey through the financial wilderness in the currency of time. For instance, if you're currently feeling completely harassed by all the demands being made on you, you might be in a State of *feel* and a Level of basic Sufficiency. Do you think within the next few minutes or hours you could move to the state of *think* and the level of Efficiency? That would mean you have stopped emoting and you're now making logical plans. It would also mean that doing so has created a situation where you have enough **time** to get everything done, even if not in a steady or predictable way.

Is that asking a lot? If so, perhaps moving one step diagonally to the right on the grid is all you can handle right now. Or do you think that by later on today, you could move through a *relax* State and into the State of *create*, where you find a new way to use **time** more efficiently? Perhaps you'll figure out how to automate a task or ask a family member to take on one of your obligations. If so, you will have moved all the way up to the intersection of *create* and Efficiency or Proficiency (or better!).

The speed at which you move around in this grid is entirely up to you. The object of the game, generally, is to move to the right when it comes to Financial States (x axis) while you also move up on the y axis of Financial Levels. You can use the grid to assess your progress and have some idea of what your next goal looks like and what you need to do to achieve it—long term or short term.

Let's do the same exercise when it comes to your currency of **health**.

Health

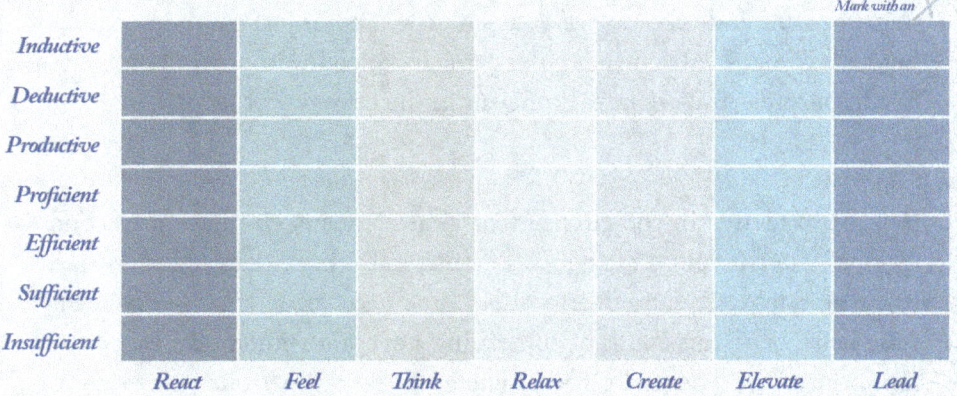

THE Y AXIS

INSUFFICIENT

If you never feel healthy and always feel sick, or if you're suffering from a debilitating illness, you're in an Insufficient state. Health also applies to mood, so if you're in a state of constant depression, you're Insufficient.

SUFFICIENT

If you sometimes feel healthy and well, sometimes have enough energy to accomplish everything, and/or are sometimes feeling positive about life, but not consistently, then you're in a Sufficient state.

EFFICIENT

If you have exactly as much energy as you need to accomplish all your daily tasks, if you fall into bed exhausted and spent, yet satisfied, every evening, you exist in a state of Efficiency. You have no margin, no extra energy for emergencies, but you're taking care of yourself and your loved ones on a day-to-day basis.

PROFICIENT

If you have a little bit of extra energy every week, that means you actually have time to make it to that dentist appointment, take those vitamins, do that workout, and take care of yourself. You are not just surviving; you're improving your health on a regular basis. Financially, improving is akin to having surplus. You are now Proficient in the currency of health.

PRODUCTIVE

Being Productive in the currency of health means you have a "second income" when it comes to energy. Because you're not exhausted every day, you're able to exert extra energy should the need arise. If someone needs your help, or if you think of something new you want to do, you have the positive attitude and physical energy to go out of your way to do it. Productivity can also mean that you're creating a health surplus by steadily improving your health with workouts, weight management, counseling, or other pro-health measures.

Unlike the currency of **stuff**, most young people begin life at a level of **health** Productivity or better. All the sports they play and the activities they do contribute to making them healthier and healthier. It's when we get older that Productivity becomes harder to achieve.

DEDUCTIVE

Deductivity in **health** means you are perfectly healthy and no longer have to pay your "**health** expenses." That means you don't worry any more about your weight, your eyesight, your hearing, your daily energy levels, your blood pressure, etcetera. You no longer have deficits in these areas because all the investments you've made into your **health** have finally paid off to make you an overall healthy person with no significant **health** challenges and energy to spare.

Young people often achieve Deductivity easily, as their growing bodies experience very few "deficits" and their boundless energy provides a second "income" of energy that can make them healthier and healthier as long as they remain active.

INDUCTIVE

Those experiencing Inductivity in the currency of **health** are, first of all, happy people. Their mental and physical **health** are paired in such a way that life just keeps getting better and better. They don't have to do much to keep this level of **health**; they are simply at the top of their game. This could describe a teenager at the peak of his or her physical development. It could also describe a pregnant woman overwhelmed with positive hormones while her body creates life itself. A champion body builder may be in an Inductive state as long as his inner **health** matches what shows on the outside. Even young children can be in a state of Inductivity as their bodies grow and their minds enjoy those "wonder years."

THE X AXIS

Disregarding, for the moment, what your essential Financial Nature happens to be, let's assess where you stand in terms of the crossroads of **health** and the Financial States. Health issues can linger for a long time or come and go quickly, so your personal progress through the States will be unique to you and your particular body/mind condition. Oftentimes, you have less control over your progress through the States in terms of health than you have in terms of stuff or time, but we all work on our health in one way or another, whether it's exercising or taking medication or simply doing the heart-centered work of accepting ourselves just the way we are.

Remember that, when it comes to your progress in the currency of health, only you can assess whether or not you're ready to move from one Financial State to the next. But typically, when you're ready, you'll know.

FEEL

When it comes to health, are you feeling a lot of emotion around it? If you get some kind of diagnosis, it's inevitable that feelings will emerge. Then again, if you reach a big weight loss goal, that might feel great! Society and the media can make us feel terrible about the health problems that show, and our doctors may reprimand us for not taking care of ourselves. As we navigate the paths toward health, it's normal to pass through the State of *feel* on a regular basis. But like with all the Financial States, the trick is not to get stuck here. Remember that your mental health is part of this, too, so if you're feeling down (or up!) this is okay so long as you're able to cycle through it and keep the wheel of States turning.

THINK

Being in a State of *think* with your health could mean you're dealing with your mental health a lot. You're "in your head." Or it could mean you're making a lot of logical plans around improving your health. The State of *think* follows *feel* because once we have experienced all the feelings around a situation, we need to step away from our feelings in order to rationally consider what to do next. In the case of your health, this could mean deciding to join a gym, see a doctor, get outdoors more, or read a self-help book. It's that decision, and the intention behind it, that gets you into the State of *think*.

RELAX

Relaxing is, of course, crucial to health. More than any other currency, the State of *relax* comes to the fore when we're talking about this currency. This point is important in the cycle of Financial States because it prevents us from taking the plans we made during *think* and making hasty decisions. When it comes to health, relaxation is doubly crucial because it actually helps build health itself. So, when you're in a State of *relax,* that doesn't mean you're necessarily chilling out on a tropical beach. It means you have made plans about how to increase your health currency and now you're taking it easy while you let the plans trickle down into your subconscious. Soon, you'll begin to *create,* but for now, you're just taking some time to pause before acting.

CREATE

The *creative* phase of the Financial States is where you take action to increase your health currency. Here, you'll create some new system, program, object, or action that takes you closer to your health goal. Being creative in terms of health could mean creating an account at a yoga studio where you plan to attend classes. It could mean creating a system for taking your medication in a more predictable way, or it could mean manifesting better health through meditation. The main thing to remember is that during this phase, you take action based upon the well-thought-out plan that was inspired by your *feelings* and tempered by the previous State of *relaxation.*

ELEVATE

When you *elevate* in the currency of health, you not only help yourself but others. The old cliche of "helping an old lady cross the street" would apply here (assuming she wanted to go that way!). Counseling a friend is also a way to contribute to the mental health of another. Even taking your cat to the vet *elevates* someone else's health while you also help yourself by getting more purrs from your furry friend. *Elevating* is important because we're all connected, most especially in the currency of health. These Covid times have been a stark reminder that the health of one can affect the health of all, so seeing your community as one body will help improve everyone's health currency.

LEAD

Leading follows *elevating* because it means helping others help themselves. In this State, you have improved your own health currency, even if just by a little bit, so you reach out to make sure others have the same opportunity. "A rising tide lifts all boats," as they say, and all it really takes to spread your little bit of success to others is to talk about it. If you have taken up a healthy pursuit, met a new guru, or found a great podiatrist, spread the word so that others can take advantage of this same opportunity. Often, gaining health currency is about learning how to care for ourselves better, so it's easy to simply share that knowledge in order to *lead*.

REACT

In the currency of health, too much time in a *reactive* State can raise blood pressure and cortisol levels. Such stress isn't good for the body or mind, nonetheless, the *reactive* State is still an important part of the cycle of Financial States. If you touch your hand to a hot stove, you better *react* without stopping to *think* or *feel* first! If you're climbing a mountain and find yourself on the edge of a steep cliff, you'll rely on your ability to *react* above all other things. *Reacting* is job number one when it comes to preserving our health because it's how we stay safe. Whenever you're in some kind of health deficit, you'll first *react*, then, once you've assessed the situation, hopefully you'll move on to *feel*. Being able to enter and exit the state of *react* without lingering there too long is key to using this State to its best advantage in the currency of health.

FINDING YOUR PLACE ON THE GRID: NOW, LATER, TODAY, AND TOMORROW

As you did when assessing the currency of time, you'll now want to go back to the grid above and mark the square where your Financial Level in the currency of health intersects with your Financial State in the currency of health, right now. As with the other currencies, our Financial States in health can change quickly, as can our Financial Levels. If you've ever felt perfectly fine and then come down with food poisoning or been seized with muscle cramps, you know how quickly you can plummet from Proficiency to Insufficiency. And if you've ever been lost in thought while driving, then suddenly had to swerve to avoid an animal in the road, you know how easy it is to jump from the state of *think* to that of *react*.

We move up, down, left, and right in this matrix all the time, all day long, which is the "small picture" view, but if you sit down with this matrix and assess the overall state of your **health** once a week or once a month, on a regular basis, hopefully you'll see yourself moving toward your goal in terms of the "big picture." The key to growth in this, as in all currencies, is to assess your current State but also know your goal. Not everyone aspires to the top right corner of the grid in all currencies. Select the place you'd like to be by the end of the day, week, or month, and if you get used to assessing where you stand on this matrix, it will help you realize if and when you're making progress in the currency of **health**. Remember, life is still about the journey! It's just that without goals and a starting place, there can be no journey.

Relationship

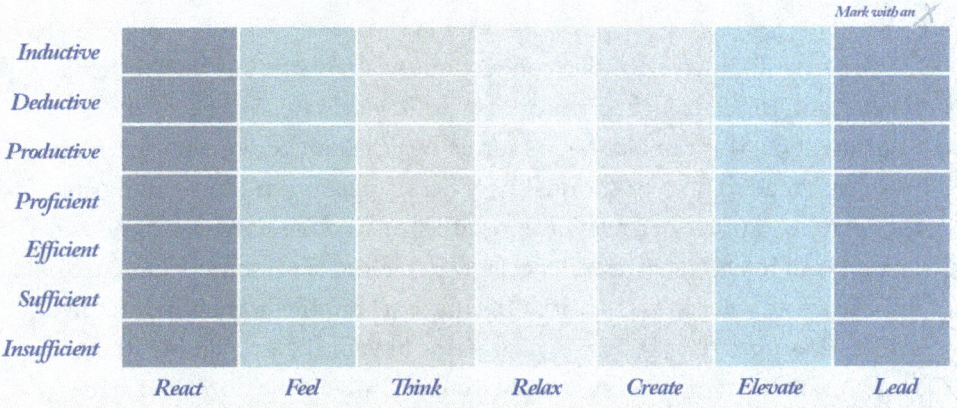

THE Y AXIS

Having viewed the Financial Levels and Financial States in terms of time and health, you probably have a good idea where we're going now: relationships. Looking at money in terms of whether you're in debt, breaking even, or well-invested is pretty logical, but when we look at our relationships that way, it's tempting to suggest that love and human connection can't be quantified: a fair point. However, we all know when we're satisfied with the relationships in our lives and when we're not. Marriage is a sign of satisfaction; divorce, of dissatisfaction. Functioning friendships are satisfying, but friendships that make you feel used or exploited are not. Caring parental figures make their offspring feel safe and loved, while a lack of the same creates a relationship deficit that can require years of therapy to heal. So, relationships can be good and bad, functional and dysfunctional, and what we want to do here is simply assess where you are in your relationships so we can help you get to where you'd like to be. The grid above can be a useful tool in that regard.

INSUFFICIENT

If you never feel you have positive, satisfying connections with others, then you're in an Insufficient state. Enough said.

SUFFICIENT

If you sometimes have positive connections with others, but they're inconsistent and unreliable, then you're in a Sufficient state. When it comes to relationships, this can also be viewed as Insufficient, because abusive relationships tend to take on the quality of being great one minute and terrible the next. So, if you're in a relationship with that kind of severe, up-and-down quality, and it feels like the roller coaster depletes your resources more than uplifting you, you can classify it as Insufficient. But if you genuinely receive satisfaction from the various relationships in your life and simply struggle to get that feeling more consistently, you're firmly in the Sufficient state.

EFFICIENT

You've reached a state of Efficiency when the **relationships** in your life feel satisfying. Things don't have to be perfect, but overall, when it comes to your important **relationships** such as parents, children, spouse, friends, and business associates, you go through life feeling functional, non-combative, and able to solve problems pretty easily. In Efficiency, you're generally improving your existing **relationships** little by little.

PROFICIENT

When it comes to money, Proficiency means you have surplus: you make more money than you spend. So when it comes to **relationships**, the same thing applies, but what does it mean to "make more **relationships**?" After all, nobody needs six hundred friends. It's better to put your energy into a few good ones. So, we don't want to "make more **relationships**" the way we "make more money." Instead, we want to make more of our existing **relationships**. Your monetary Financial Level can be assessed by a banker, the amount of quality **time** you enjoy can be seen on your daily planner entries, and **health** can be assessed with medical tests, but the quality of your **relationships** is entirely subjective and can only be determined by you, so let's talk about how to assess that.

Another important factor enters the equation at this level, which is: What do we mean by "surplus" when it comes to **relationships**? Unlike money, you can't "save" your **relationships** in a rainy-day fund. **Relationships** are in-the-moment, ongoing experiences and daily exercises in give and take. So when it comes to surplus in this currency, you want to ask yourself, "Do I have enough love and support that I can afford to give away more than I receive?" If your relationship life enables you to reach out to others in need by offering a genuine hug or listening ear, you are no longer just barely keeping things together. You're secure enough in yourself that you have surplus. This currency is impossible to save. You spend your love and caring as soon as you feel it. That's how you know you have surplus.

PRODUCTIVE

Productivity, when it comes to money, means you've invested in such a way that you receive dividends. Are you receiving dividends from your

relationships? Remember, relationship currency can't be saved. It has to be spent in order to exist, so dividends represent love and caring that is being actively given and received. Has the **time** and energy you put into your **relationships** resulted in free-flowing love and appreciation that makes you prone to give even more?

Every relationship is different, so it's possible some of your **relationships** are yielding great dividends while others … not so much. This happens frequently, as people often have to choose which **relationships** to spend **time** nurturing. That said, being in a state of Productivity means the **relationships** that matter the most to you are yielding such dividends that you can give to them more than you receive.

Good **relationships** provide a sense of being loved and cared for by other individuals but also a sense that we live in a supportive community which will uplift us in the event of emergency. If you enjoy a "second income" in this currency, that is equivalent to a "second outflow." It means you're not just sharing love, respect, and caring with those in your immediate orbit but reaching out to share with the greater community and making yourself part of a safety net that benefits all.

DEDUCTIVE

The difference between the Deductive Level and the Productive Level is a simple matter of having eliminated debt. This begs the question: what is "debt" in **relationship** currency? In money, it's clear that you can have both income and debts at the same time, but when it comes to **relationships**, don't we eliminate debts when we do what it takes to build up our stockpile of currency? One way to look at this is to simply realize that we may be in "relationship debt" to some people even while we're in a state of surplus with others. So, at this level, we have taken stock of each and every one of our **relationships** and brought them all into a state of surplus or free-flowing love and acceptance on both sides.

INDUCTIVE

Inductivity with money means you no longer have to work for cash. The investments you have made produce enough dividends to pay all your debts and give you plenty to live on. But with **relationships**, there's no such thing as "no longer working." **Relationships** require constant attention and upkeep. Hopefully it doesn't feel like work, but let's face it, problems arise in life and we have to work them out with people. That simply never ends, no matter how "enlightened" you may become. But remember that with the currency of **relationship**, saving is impossible: there is only giving and receiving. So living off of a "second income" in this case means you now receive love and caring from people you have never met. You have, by now, given so much to your community, company, country, or planet, that complete strangers offer you their love, acceptance, caring, and support.

Some would say fame puts people in a state of Inductivity, as it causes them to receive lots of love and appreciation from strangers. This is the case only when their personal life is also yielding the same results. The appearance of being beloved by all is not true Inductivity. This state is only reached by building your relationship resources from the ground up and keeping them strong both at the core and the extremities.

THE X AXIS

On the x axis of the chart above, we assess how our **relationships** are doing in terms of the Financial States. By now you understand that these are the States we need to pass through, in order, if we want to improve our standing in the Financial Level of the currency in question. These states have a lot to do with our relationship with ourselves—our own hearts and minds; so, more than any other currency, it's clear how the Financial States relate to the currency of **relationship**.

FEEL

Whether you're considering one particular relationship or all your **relationships** as a group, when you're in an intense state of *feeling*—whether it's good or bad—you're experiencing the Financial State of *feel*. It's important to be aware of your feelings but a mistake to get stuck here. Remember that healthy **relationships** are about more than just feelings. Be sure to keep cycling through all the States.

THINK

Relationships are problem-solving adventures. Once you've observed your feelings, the next phase with any particular relationship is to *think* about how to increase that currency. If it's already great, then just enjoy the feeling and hang out in the *feel* State a bit longer! You can apply the *think* state to any relationship that needs to be improved.

RELAX

Acting in a hasty manner can be the biggest mistake in any relationship, so the State of *relax* is a crucial stopping point in any interaction. Having *thought* about how to increase your relationship currency, take a step back and enjoy a relaxing cup of tea or a comfortable stretch. Just let your decision gel in your brain a while before taking action. We've all seen (and been) that person who sends a badly worded email or leaves a phone message in the heat of the moment, only to regret it later. Now is the time to prevent that from happening again! Stop. *Relax.*

CREATE

Creating, in relationship currency, can mean making a new friend or building a new type of connection with an associate. It could mean asking someone to marry you or having a baby. *Create* is the phase where we take action to build something new, and that might be a small action or something life-altering. Creativity is the key to both building new relationships and solving problems, so this is where you take bold action!

ELEVATE

When we *elevate*, we lift up others along with ourselves. We create systems (like families and friend groups) that make life easier for everyone. When you *elevate* your relationships, you seek new ways to serve others rather than take from them. You enjoy giving, teaching, and providing. Some would argue that being a parent is the ultimate *elevating* activity, as the only way to succeed is to help your children succeed. But there are many situations where one might feel parental towards another or simply be inclined to help for innumerable reasons. These all qualify as *elevating*.

LEAD

A *leader* in the currency of **relationship** is just that. More than any other currency, **relationships** define leaders by enabling them to guide others toward success. True leaders don't do things for their followers, don't give things to their followers, don't enable followers to indulge in selfishness—rather, they teach others how to provide **relationship** currency for themselves. *Leaders* show by example how to both accept and provide love and caring to others and how to live in an enlightened space of win-win problem solving.

REACT

Let's face it, being emotionally *reactive* can be terrible for a lot of **relationships**. Typically, as we mature, we learn to breathe through our periods of *reactivity* and move into an awareness of our feelings so that we can solve problems rather than explode with emotion. But the State of *react* helps build **relationships** by allowing us to express emotion in what might, frankly, be a less civilized manner than what you're going to do in later States. Also, the expression of love and passion is purest from those deeply in a state of *react*, where their actions don't bother to pass through a filter of awareness or logic, first.

For some, the State of *react* is easy to enter and hard to leave. Alcohol and drugs can cause us to stagnate in the State of *react* without enabling our other States to kick in, and this causes serious relationship problems. Intoxicants can also create a good-feeling illusion of love and warmth that sadly doesn't last. On the other hand, some people are very controlled by nature and find it difficult to enter the state of *react* at all. Primal scream therapy was created for individuals like these. Such therapies give us permission to simply *react* to our relationship troubles in a safe space. The most important thing about the State of *react*, as it relates to the **relationship** currency, is that it's natural, normal, and valuable, but to build lasting **relationships**, it's crucial to keep on cycling through the States.

FINDING YOUR PLACE ON THE GRID: NOW, LATER, TODAY, AND TOMORROW

By now, you know the drill. Go ahead and assess where you are in your overall relationship currency in terms of both the Financial Levels on the y axis and the Financial States on the x axis. If you like, you can even place a unique mark on the grid for each important relationship in your life.

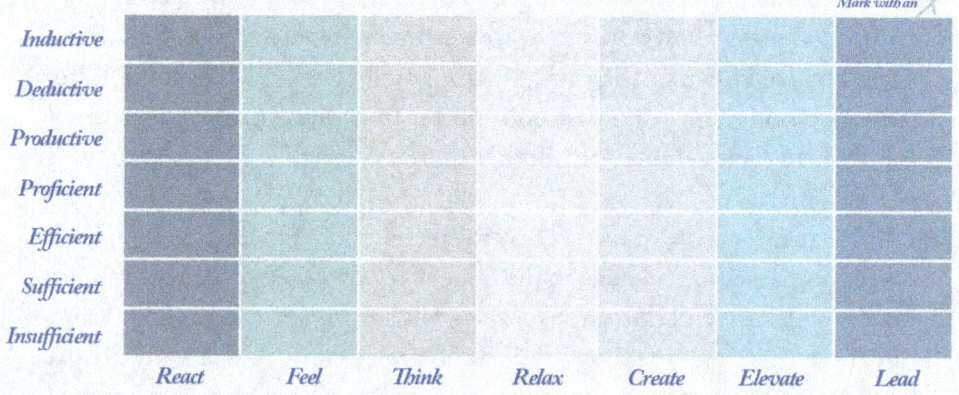

Mark with an X

	React	Feel	Think	Relax	Create	Elevate	Lead
Inductive							
Deductive							
Productive							
Proficient							
Efficient							
Sufficient							
Insufficient							

THE Y AXIS

I have already gone over the basics of how this matrix works when it comes to **stuff** (my word for lumping together money with the things it can buy). So I'll be brief as I walk you through the same process with a view to finding your place on the above grid.

INSUFFICIENT

If you never have enough money to take care of your basic needs, if you're always in debt and can't see any way out, then you're in an Insufficient state.

SUFFICIENT

If you sometimes have enough money, but your income tends to fluctuate up and down unpredictably, you're in a state of Sufficiency with your **stuff**.

EFFICIENT

If your income and debts are perfectly aligned but leave you no surplus, this describes a state of Efficiency.

PROFICIENT

When you make more money than you spend, that means you have surplus. If you have not taken the step of investing that surplus but are simply enjoying it, you're at a level called Proficient.

PRODUCTIVE

At the Productive Level, you have taken your surplus and invested it in order to receive dividends, or a second income for which you don't have to work.

DEDUCTIVE

When that second income is so great that it regularly pays off your debts and monthly bills, you are in Deductivity.

INDUCTIVE

Inductivity occurs when your second income has become so great that you no longer have to work for a living. Your investments cover your bills and daily expenses while also contributing to the investments themselves.

THE X AXIS

Here, we look at our relationship with **stuff** as it applies to the Financial States.

FEEL

If you're in an emotional place with money—either panicking, worrying, or rejoicing—you're in a State of *feel*.

THINK

The State of *think* describes people who are actively working on ways to improve their financial lives—not necessarily taking action but making serious plans and engaging in problem-solving exercises.

RELAX

Those in a State of *relax* have passed through the *think* stage and are taking a moment (or day or week) to sit with the ideas and information and make sure they feel good about the plans they've made.

CREATE

In the *create* State, you're at your most creative, actively engaging in problem-solving activities and building whatever new things are needed to make your vision of the future happen.

ELEVATE

Having created something new, you're now ready to bring others along on your successful ride. The State of *elevate* is where you make your brilliant creation into something that uplifts some aspect of the community rather than just yourself.

LEAD

When you *lead*, you share the wealth. Those in this phase aren't necessarily wealthy philanthropists. In fact, they might still be at the beginning stages of their financial journeys, but to move to the next Level, they'll find some way to help others in the community help themselves to the resources needed to succeed.

REACT

The State of *react* is an essential aspect of every financial journey. It means you now see a new situation that needs to be remedied and you're exploring the instincts that accompany that realization. It's the last stage of a successful financial journey but also the first stage of your next journey.

FINDING YOUR PLACE ON THE GRID: NOW, LATER, TODAY, AND TOMORROW

In many ways, **stuff** is the easiest of the four currencies to quantify. It can be relatively easy to mark your Financial Level on the y axis, but then you must decide which State you're currently in on the x axis. Knowing exactly which square you occupy on this grid will will help you see how much you have achieved already, along with the goal ahead.

Hopefully, at this point, you you understand how the four currencies play roles in your life. You've learned how to assess the Level of each currency in terms of the seven Financial Levels I have presented to you. Often, people assess their **time**, **stuff**, **relationships**, and **health** by saying they're good, bad, better than before, declining, improving, or using other vague terms, but with these seven Levels, you now have a much more accurate and descriptive way to categorize exactly where you are in each currency as well as set goals for what stage you'd like to achieve next.

I hope you understand how crucial it is to cycle through the Financial States in each currency. Getting stuck in one State for a very long time is the cause of stagnation, but consciously urging yourself to move through the cycle helps you achieve your goals, whatever they may be. Your Financial Nature is the only part of this program that's fixed. The Levels and States can and must change as you grow and improve through life.

As we discussed earlier, the States are like the long hand on an analog clock, which moves at a steady pace through each minute, while the short hand (here representing the Financial Levels) seems to stand still. Then, finally, when the long hand has completed its circuit around the clock, we realize that the short hand was moving in tiny increments all along, and now it has progressed to the next number on the clock, the next hour. The way the short hand moves one notch every hour is analogous to how one moves steadily forward in Financial Levels as long as one keeps the long hand, the Financial States, moving steadily along, never stagnating.

Now that you've marked your places on all the grids above, go ahead and also mark a square on each matrix to represent where you aspire to be in a given period of time. You can decide for yourself whether you're setting goals for the day, week, month, or year.

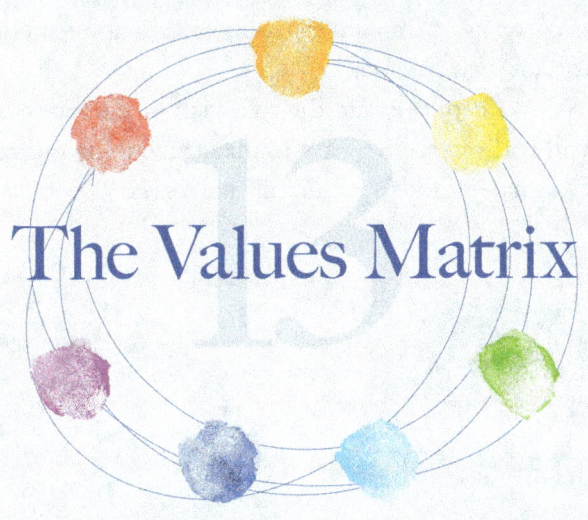

The Values Matrix

WHEN YOU CATEGORIZE the elements of your life into the four currencies, you'll notice that each currency comes into play in several different aspects of life. For instance, when considering the currency of time, we have to manage it as part of our work lives. For this we have day planners and calendars. We also have to manage time when we play. For this, we use timers when playing sports and metronomes when playing music. Even children who can't tell time use the setting of the sun to know when it's time to go inside. We also manage time when we relax. For instance, we may take a catnap for a brief moment in-between two obligations, letting the timing of those other experiences assign time currency to our relaxation. Finally, we manage time when we're pursuing our passions such as volunteerism or creative expression. Those of us drawn to certain passions often wish we could do these things all day every day, but responsibly

Even a soul submerged in sleep is hard at work and helps make something of the world

HERACLITUS

managing the currency of **time** means using self discipline to limit the **time** we get to spend on such passions.

In order to do a deep dive into the role each of the four currencies play in our lives and really examine ways to maximize these currencies, I view each currency as having four specific subcategories:

TIME

➤ *Work*   ➤ *Relax*
➤ *Play*   ➤ *Passion*

HEALTH

➤ *Energy*   ➤ *Mental*
➤ *Nutrition*   ➤ *Social*

RELATIONSHIPS

➤ *Self*   ➤ *Family*
➤ *Partner*   ➤ *Friends*

STUFF

➤ *Money*   ➤ *Auto*
➤ *Home*   ➤ *Things*

One way to quantify the status of each category of each currency is to simply assign a number between one and seven to your satisfaction with, for example:

> *"The time I get to spend not thinking about any of my obligations"* **(time:** *relax)*

> *"The happiness I feel from hanging out with friends"* **(health:** *social)*

> *"The level of trust I share with my children"* **(relationships:** *family)*

> *"How reliable is my vehicle?"* **($tuff:** *auto)*

The numbers one through seven correspond to the seven Financial Levels. In order to recall in detail which number best describes your status in each subcategory, see the description of the Financial Levels starting on page 129. Or simply refer to figure 16 on page 139:

Here is a table you can use to note how each subcategory plays a role in your life and what satisfaction number you assign to it. Ignore the rightmost column for now.

Currency/ subcurrency	In your own words
TIME: WORK	
TIME: PLAY	
TIME: RELAX	
TIME: PASSION	

Current Financial Level (1 to 7)	Desired Financial Level (1 to 7)	Current point on Wheel of Financial States

Currency/ subcurrency	In your own words
HEALTH: ENERGY	
HEALTH: NUTRITION	
HEALTH: MENTAL	
HEALTH: SOCIAL	

Current Financial Level (1 to 7)	Desired Financial Level (1 to 7)	Current point on Wheel of Financial States

Currency/ subcurrency	In your own words
RELATIONSHIPS: SELF	
RELATIONSHIPS: PARTNER	
RELATIONSHIPS: FAMILY	
RELATIONSHIPS: FRIENDS	

Current Financial Level (1 to 7)	Desired Financial Level (1 to 7)	Current point on Wheel of Financial States

Currency/ subcurrency	In your own words
$TUFF: MONEY	
$TUFF: HOME	
$TUFF: AUTO	
$TUFF: THINGS	

Current Financial Level (1 to 7)	*Desired Financial Level (1 to 7)*	*Current point on Wheel of Financial States*

With these numbers in place, we have a more detailed view of the location of our currencies on our financial MAP, don't we? We know exactly where we are on each of our journeys. But just marking where you currently are and your destination doesn't fulfill a map's intended use. A map must also show the path for getting from point A to point B. We've learned that our COMPASS, a.k.a. The Financial States is the tool we use to figure out the next step to take toward a goal, so let's add something to our table above: the wheel of Financial States, as seen below and in the rightmost column of the table above.

FIGURE 18

In each currency subcategory, you can mark where you currently are on the wheel of Financial States. This way, the next step in order for you to make progress will be obvious: simply complete your task in your current Financial State and consciously direct yourself into the next one on the wheel.

Summing Up part 5:
Your Guidebook

With this background information, let's take a look at the Evolution Matrix again, so you can really see yourself as a traveler in this great big wilderness of financial planning. Before, we assessed the progress of our fictional hero Freddie Freespirit on this three-dimensional matrix. Now, go ahead and use the assessments you made on the **time**, **health**, **relationship**, and **stuff** grids and transfer those marks over to this 3D-looking model. Also use a different mark to note your goals for each currency on the matrix.

Now you truly have a map that will get you through the financial wilderness. Use this matrix as the image that shows where you are, where you want to be, and the step-by-step path to getting there. You should understand the importance of passing through each of the Financial States in order to get ahead. Don't skip any of the States as you make progress. You know how they say, "There is no shortcut to success?" Well, this map illustrates that fact perfectly. You simply can't skip over any of these important States as you work toward success in what matters most to you.

PART 6

Boots On The Ground

*Tis not too late to seek
a newer world*

HERACLITUS

Applying the Financial Levels to Organizations

MANY ARE FAMILIAR with what is commonly called the Serenity Prayer:

God grant me the serenity to accept the things I cannot change, courage to change the things I can, and wisdom to know the difference

The system I have taught you so far is meant to provide the key to financial serenity: "the wisdom to know the difference." For instance, your Financial Nature is fixed. Your Financial Level, for the time being, is also fixed, but you have the ability to change that Level by using the one aspect of this program where you have the power to make change: The Financial States.

You can will yourself to take the action needed to move from one Financial State to the next. This will ultimately change your Financial Level, but never your base Financial Nature, however when you do this enough you will build financial habits that allow you to act as if your Nature has changed.

Understanding the COMPASS in this book is crucial because most people go through life with a sense that they can't change their Financial Level, although they want to. Ambitious people cast about for new ways to invest or gamble or get better jobs or take on side work or gain notoriety—always seeking the key to getting unstuck from the Financial Level in which they are mired. The mistake they make is failing to see that there isn't one action that moves you up to the next level. Instead, it's a seven-step process, as I've outlined above, where you need to recognize the psychological State you're in, fulfil that State, then consciously jump to the next State when the time is right.

With each movement from State to State, there is likely to be some discomfort. Often, you're asking yourself to do something unfamiliar. But, of course, if there were no discomfort, you would have figured out how to make financial progress all by yourself and you wouldn't even need this book. Helping you see that the discomfort it necessary but temporary is a big part of what this book should do for you.

Now that you've learned all about how to set a PURPOSE, understand your SELF, view the financial MAP, and make progress on that map, you can move ahead in your own financial life. But our individual financial lives are just microcosms of the world at large. Families, companies, non-profits, civic agencies, and entire governments follow the same patterns and get stuck in the same ways as individuals. The next section will talk about the Financial Natures, Levels, and States from just such a big-picture perspective.

How Financial Levels are Misunderstood

It's important to understand this system of Financial Levels because when people don't know how very high they can go, and therefore how easy the acquisition of money can be in the Inductive phase, they tend never to get there. But this is often because they don't even know that the higher levels—where your life is fueled by passive income—are an achievable option.

Typically, once someone has reached a level of Proficiency, where some surplus exists, they think they've "made it." They spend that surplus until their income and expenses are perfectly aligned again, which brings them back down to the level of Efficiency. This new spending habit may further cause them to descend to the level of simple Sufficiency, and finally back down to Insufficiency. At this point, people usually realize their spending is out of control, so they work hard to get back up to Sufficiency, then Efficiency, and they feel pretty good about themselves when they finally make it to Proficiency again, where they have surplus cash. Then, they spend the cash just as before. The cycle looks like this:

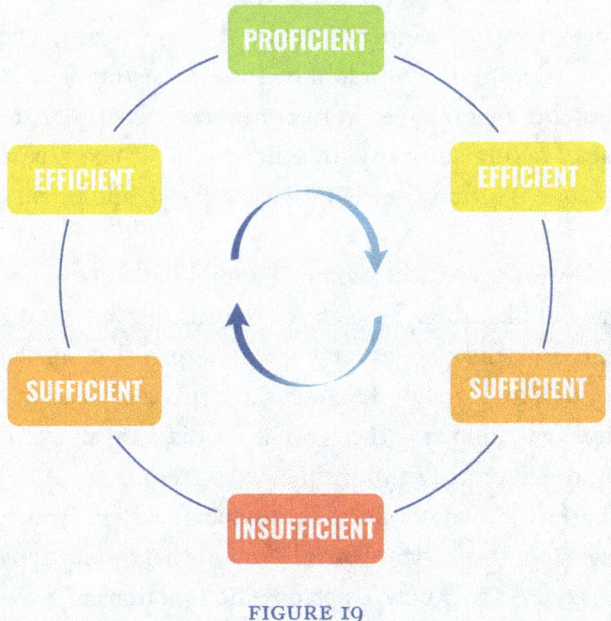

FIGURE 19

Do you notice that in the above diagram, the higher Financial Levels of Productivity, Deductivity, and Inductivity have been cut out of the process? Not knowing about—and therefore not even striving for—those higher levels dooms folks to a situation where retirement is impossible. At these first four levels, if you want to keep making income, you have to keep working.

Making that jump from Proficiency, where you have surplus income, to Productivity, where you invest instead of spend that surplus in order to get a secondary income that requires no work—this is the key to getting off that endless wheel of work. It's amazing how many people don't understand the importance of this transition. What's even more amazing is how many institutions, companies, and governments equally fail to understand it. Let me give you an example.

My Local School Board

For many years, I was a member of my local school board, where I helped determine the allocation of tax dollars. In our meetings—and in taxpayer-funded systems generally—a commonly held belief is that surplus is a sign of abuse of taxing authority. In other words, if taxes have brought in more money than is strictly needed, that money should be returned to the taxpayers.

Doing so, however, results in making it impossible to engage in long-range, prudent financial planning. To plan for the future, you need investments that will yield dividends; so, as long as you return that surplus instead of investing it, you'll go through the exact same funds-allocation process year after year after year, following the cycle in the diagram above. There will be no growth or development in your financial system.

In the first few levels of a personal financial system, you typically get money by working. In a civic financial system, that money typically comes through taxation. As we know, a person who functions in a system limited only to the phases of Insufficiency, Sufficiency, Efficiency, and Proficiency (levels 1-4) is working away like a hamster on an exercise wheel, never achieving a Level where they can rest. By the same token, a civic organization that functions like this is continually taxing people like that same busy hamster. But there is another way. Take a look at the diagram below:

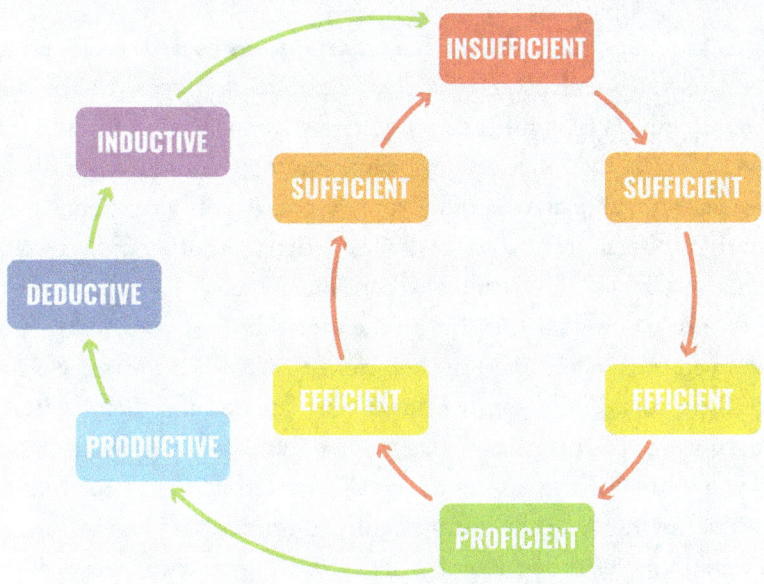

FIGURE 20

Imagine starting at Insufficiency and traveling clockwise. With good funds allocation, you move through Sufficiency and Efficiency all the way to the level of Proficiency where you have surplus income. From here, you have two choices—you can use investment to follow the green arrows and ascend further to the levels of Productivity, Deductivity, and Inductivity, or you can return the surplus money to the taxpayers, not invest it, and follow the red arrows right back to simple Efficiency, where there is no surplus at all. Many civic organizations go around and around the red wheel and never choose to invest their surplus, build their wealth, and ascend to the point where taxes will ultimately be unnecessary. But institutions often fail to see it this way.

Many civic planners actually have a conscious goal of going through the tax-and-spend process shown in the red wheel, year after year after year. As elected officials, it is their job to allocate taxpayer monies, so when they return surplus funds to taxpayers, this makes them look (in the short run) like wonderfully efficient organizers and leads to their annual re-election because they "save so much money."

But taking the long view of the situation, it's easy to see the benefit of investing the surplus funds so that the following year the investment will pay dividends that fill the city coffers without having to take it from taxpayers. With such investments, civic planners could eventually lower and even eliminate taxes overall by going forward from Proficiency through Productivity, Deductivity, and finally Inductivity. Another option would be to both invest surplus funds and also continue to tax at the same rate—that's a lot of funds coming in! Imagine all the incredible civic projects that could be achieved with such ongoing community wealth building. Sovereign wealth funds in certain countries have been created that help to illustrate this example of civic planning. Private schools and corporations do it as well. There is a name for the failure to see this pattern. I call it the "efficiency addiction." It shows up in innumerable organizations. For instance, the supply-chain issues brought on by the Covid-19 pandemic were caused by a world addicted to simple efficiency.

The Choice to Return to Insufficiency

Viewing the diagram, you'll notice that, either way, the cycle always brings you back to Insufficiency, but once you have taken the Productivity path, your return to Insufficiency will not mean poverty. In this case, Insufficiency means you have recognized a new need you'd like to fulfill. In the case of a school board, if you have filled your coffers with dividends from your investments and no longer have to tax the public, the new Insufficiency you recognize may be a need to update infrastructure, train teachers on multiple learning styles, or establish a satellite school focused on STEM, the arts, or trades. Once you have the funds to start dreaming bigger, that new dream becomes your new Insufficiency, and the cycle begins again—only this time, you may be interested in building one of the other four currencies.

The Choice to Avoid Insufficiency

Many organizations are stuck somewhere in-between the choice to revolve endlessly on the red wheel and the potential progress they could make by following the green path. These organizations wisely invest their surplus but have a Protector motivation style. They have the money to change but fear the upheaval that could come with allocating funds to big projects. Philosophically, they even fear the new ideas that come from updating a school system in order to embrace the latest advances in pedagogy. Here is the diagram they follow:

When you arrive at **PROFICIENT**, *you can choose the fork in the road that goes up and to the left or back down and to the right.*

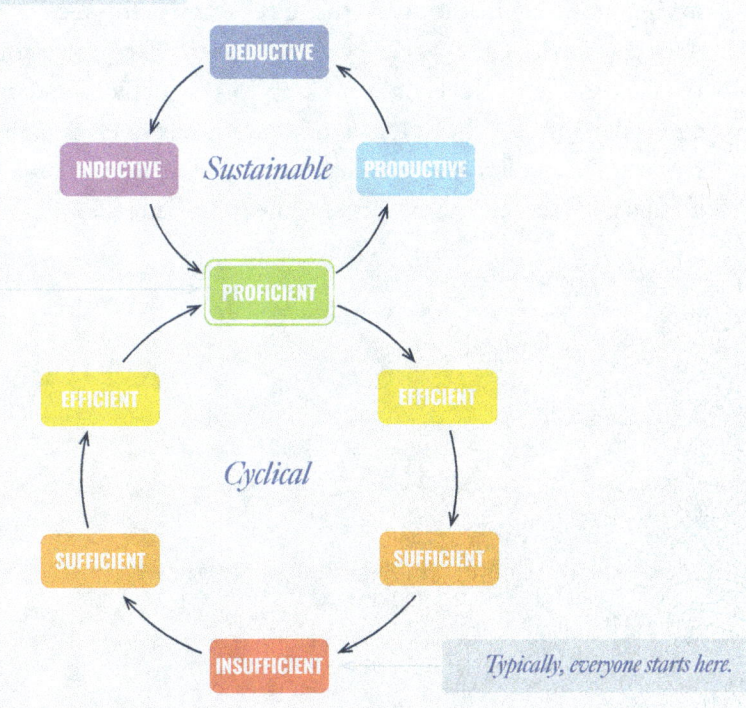

FIGURE 21

Starting at Insufficiency, they rise to Proficiency, where they have to choose whether they'll invest their surplus in order to rise to the Productive level or return the surplus to taxpayers and cycle back down toward Insufficiency again. If they choose to invest, they rise to the top circle, where they move through the lucrative phases of Productivity, Deductivity, and Inductivity. At Inductivity, the organization can live off of its investments. At this point, an eager, forward-thinking organization might apply the red and green model above and invest what they have in a civic project to improve the lifestyles and prospects of its citizens, thus ending up right back at Insufficiency. However, if the organization chooses not to take big steps but rather maintain the status quo, will keep cycling around the "sustainable" wheel.

Instead of taking the big adventure that is Insufficiency, they'll simply cycle down to Proficiency, where regular income is always assured. As can be seen in the diagram, when any person or organization achieves the groundwork of having profitable investments, the lowest they will typically ever go again is down to the stage of Proficiency. As long as they keep investing their surplus, they'll cycle from there right back up to Productivity and avoid that lower circle altogether. When all a community needs to do is maintain the status quo, this conservative approach is perfect. A person or organization can go around and around that top wheel many times before deciding to plunge again into Insufficiency and begin a new project.

Financial Gurus and their Natures

Don't Postpone Joy

I TAKE A "DON'T postpone joy" attitude toward financial management, and for this I rely on something called leverage. Having learned my system, at least in theory, you understand how to navigate through the financial wilderness, always directed toward the goal most attractive to you. If you have carefully read the information about the Lever Financial Nature, you may already understand that life is about making trade-offs. That means no single asset or debt stands alone in value until you see it in the context of the big picture.

To increase our currency, Levers always look at ways we can manipulate our assets and debts to come out ahead. When you cycle through the wheel of Financial States, you go through the impulsive and emotional States—this is important to stay in tune with your goals—then eventually find yourself at the stage where you create something new and use it to elevate or "leverage" your positives against your negatives to improve your life's currencies in a balanced way. One of the reasons I talk about all four currencies in this book is that I have a strong belief in enjoying a balanced life as much as possible. Everything I do as a financial planner, for clients, is designed to help them solve financial problems without sacrificing the other currencies or the enjoyment of life.

Getting into debt doesn't mean you're a bad person, and you don't deserve punishment for it. Just like everyone on this Earth, you deserve a good education in problem-solving methods as well as the right to engage in problem solving while still enjoying the aspects of life that aren't a problem. That's what well-managed finances look like. In most cases, there's no sense letting financial debts ruin your **relationships**, good times, or physical comfort, even as you strive to eliminate them.

Even what those with the greatest reputation for knowing it all claim to understand and defend are but opinions

HERACLITUS

Not all financial gurus agree with this viewpoint, so I'd like to respectfully discuss some of the other popular beliefs about financial management circulating today and what underlying beliefs inspire them. My own financial nature is Lever, and I think that shows in my philosophy. Meanwhile, other gurus embody philosophies consistent with the other six Financial Natures, which explains a lot about why they see the world the way they do. In the end, I believe they each add something to the discussion that is positive and uplifting. Where I take issue with them is often with what they decide to take issue with. In other words, I have a distortion with their distortions. You'll see what I mean.

Suze Orman

A great example of a Spender, Orman uses as a guiding principle the phrase: "You are worth far more than your money." This approach toward money management is very feelings-oriented—a typical Spender viewpoint. Her attitude is compassionate and directed toward helping people gain control over their financial lives. In fact, she makes it a point, in her books and lectures, to discuss the psychological and spiritual power money wields over our lives and advises people as to how to make peace with that.

Orman asks debt sufferers to examine their behavior in the past in order to unlock keys to their financial futures, their tendencies, and the psychological roadblocks they face as they strive for financial freedom. Orman talks about facing one's fears, trusting oneself, and opening oneself up to receiving abundance. This gentle, psychological approach is exactly what I'd expect from a Spender.

Orman prompts people to examine their expenditures, cut back, and exercise discipline in order to redirect income—little bits at a time—toward better uses. She also teaches that one should pay debts off in the order of highest interest rate first, no matter the dollar amount of each individual debt. It's an approach designed to avoid emotionally overwhelming debtors but instead gradually ease them into saving more, spending less, and developing better financial habits.

Orman is also a big believer in automating your savings and retirement investment contributions, as am I. The key to the Deductive Financial Level, after all, is not wealth itself. Being in Deductivity means debt payments and second-income generation are both automated so that your lifestyle is one of enjoying whatever surplus you have, whether a lot or a little, rather than fretting over an onslaught of bills.

Generally speaking, I don't disagree with Orman's gentle, feelings-based approach to improving one's Financial Level while still living your life. There are instances, however (and the internet is full of them) when Suze overreacts or fails to do her homework. There's a bit of "Do as I say, not as I do," and sometimes "Do as I say now, not as I said before and still don't do." All financial gurus have a Nature. Like the rest of us, they are not perfect, and they struggle along the path of life, too, no matter the Level they achieve or the State in which they exist at any given time.

Dave Ramsey

In terms of financial strategy, Orman has always stood at odds with Dave Ramsey, another popular financial guru today. Their "feud" as to best financial strategies shows a profound difference in the way the different Natures think. While Orman is a feelings-oriented Spender, Ramsey's approach is that of a Lever. Like Orman, he teaches people to calculate their assets against their debts, but Ramsey's system is so logical and mathematical that, to some degree, it stagnates at the Financial States of *think*, *relax*, *create*, and *elevate* (and often skips *relax* as well as *react* and *feel*).

He teaches debtors that *reacting* and *feeling* are errors that got them into their current financial problems and should be avoided at all costs. Unlike Orman, Ramsey suggests debtors put their comfort, convenience, and pleasures on hold and live frugal, coldly calculated financial lifestyles so they can return to a pleasurable way of living once debt has been eradicated like the plague. One of Ramsey's signature strategies for this is something he calls the "Debt Snowball."

Dave Ramsey

I'm a certified financial planner, so naturally I know more about financial instruments than the average person. This book has, so far, given you only the philosophical underpinnings of the type of leverage I recommend, not a thorough understanding of the actual financial instruments you might use to achieve that leverage. Dear reader, that information will arrive at the next level up in your studies, but the story I'm going to tell in the next chapter will give you a great understanding of just how that type of leverage is achieved in a boots-on-the-ground manner, so stay tuned.

When you learn how to leverage debts against assets, you'll see that keeping your head above water is about playing it smart, not suffering.

He suggests people list their debts in order of amount, smallest debts first. Then, he recommends that while paying the minimum necessary on each debt and bill, people should direct all surplus funds toward paying off that first, smallest debt. Rather than focusing on the interest rate of each debt as the deciding factor, he believes the psychological benefit of paying off the smallest debt in its entirety is more important because it motivates the debtor to stick with the program. Ramsey believes that seeing debts disappear, one by one, is paramount because the basic tenet of his system is to live with extreme frugality until financial independence has been achieved. People need strong motivators in order to do this. "All debt is evil!" seems to appeal to his flock.

As a Lever myself, I see where Ramsey is coming from in his attempt to discipline debtors into straightening out their financial lives. Adding assets and reducing debts is the name of the game. He's got that right. But he doesn't take into account the fact that people need balance in their lives all the time, even when they're in debt. When we take the Ramsey approach, we let every other currency in our lives go out of balance simply in order to eradicate that devil known as debt.

I disagree with this approach for the reason of maintaining sanity and balance throughout life, but also because viewing debt as evil is a very bad idea. It's not debt that causes people problems; it's the interest they pay on that debt. After all, if you could take out a loan at 0% interest and pay it back as gradually as you like, why would that be a problem?

For me, the act of financial planning is all about using knowledge of the financial instruments available to help people reduce the interest rates on their debts so they can pay them off gradually without a lot of stress, preferably through automated payments.

John C. Bogle

The late Jack Bogle, author of *The Little Book of Common Sense Investing*, is known as the founder of index investing. His investment advice centered on going with the flow and not trying to reinvent any wheels. "You can't beat the market, so don't even try!" was his motto as he encouraged investors to put their money into S &P 500 index funds with their average 8% to 10% annual returns.

While many mutual fund managers claim to be able to "beat the market" with their carefully selected and timed stock pics, few ever really do, so Bogle's advice to eschew the advice of professional stock-pickers and stick with a known winner was conservative but well-informed. It was also the approach of a typical, hard-working, disciplined Earner. Earners are famous for allocating their money and time with great efficiency, as Bogle did.

The founder of Vanguard, Bogle is credited with creating the index investing strategy, whose simplicity and resulting popularity eventually made him re-think the system itself. It is said that on his deathbed, Bogle considered the financial landscape he had helped create and realized that the sheer popularity of index investing had reduced the role of professional money managers to such a degree that it made the market unhealthy.

At this point, managers were no longer exercising their skills to determine the right prices for stocks and the best places to invest. Because of this, the largest companies now received more than their fair share of capital, which could eventually cause a recession. With that recession, investors would be more likely to sell their stocks, thus introducing volatility to what was normally a very stable market.

Efficient investing hopes to guarantee a steady rate of return so that there is less chance of loss, which scares people out of the market. Earners and Savers love the implied guarantee in this "safe" approach. At Proficiency (the next level up) one's income exceeds expenses over the long term, generating surplus, which is, of course, the goal of any investment. In the beginning, Bogle's system generated Proficiency for his followers, but after it became popular, the investments being made in this country became unbalanced, favoring larger corporations and making them larger still, while smaller, less reliable funds foundered. This was caused by taking the "pro" out of Proficiency. Bogle's system eliminated the influence of the very PROfessionals who kept the American investment landscape diverse.

Naturally, I acknowledge the wisdom of investing in reliable funds such as the S&P 500, but Bogle was right when he looked at the changes his simplistic system had wrought. In point of fact, his money-focused system had ignored the currency of relationship that exists between these funds and the different companies that make up the American investment landscape. A strong emphasis on all four currencies, the seven Natures, and the three Motivations is imperative to keep Bogle's index investing approach from destabilizing markets.

Tony Robbins

Tony Robbins is both a financial coach and a self-help guru in the general sense, but in either capacity he's a great example of the Giver Nature. Givers are an interesting bunch, because while the name seems to imply they support others unconditionally, they can also fail in their ongoing efforts toward leadership. Largely, this has to do with the fact that many Givers have yet to develop the art of listening. Instead of giving people what they actually want, amateur Givers give people what they want the other person to have, which is tantamount to a type of manipulation. In his work, Robbins manages to overcome that pitfall.

Robbins' book *Awaken the Giant Within* teaches people how to use neuro-associative conditioning to train their brains to make the life changes they seek. The idea is to take certain actions in order to purposely weaken existing, unhealthy neuro-associations and take different actions to strengthen the neuro-associations you wish to have. It's kind of like training your own brain, the way you might train a dog, by giving yourself positive reinforcement for preferred behavior. This book also delves into the importance of mastering your life's emotional patterns as well as your physical well-being, time, and relationships, along with your financial life.

In his financial advice, Robbins advocates for setting up ten percent of your income to be automatically invested in savings and hiring a financial coach to manage the rest of your surplus. I certainly can't argue with that. This advice is nowhere near as complex as what you might get from a guru who is entirely financially focused, but it is not wrong.

I agree with Robbins' approach and his emphasis on finding balance with life's many currencies, as well as coming to grips with one's emotional life as part and parcel of the overall process of currency management. He doesn't address the complexities of leveraging and investment or Financial Levels, Natures, and States, as his system has a different emphasis than mine, but truly Robbins' book is an excellent complement to the information I have presented here.

Among many differences between Robbins' work and mine, though, is a sense that Robbins remains the center of his problem-solving world. This book (and his larger work as a motivational speaker and author) tends to set him up as a guru. Hiring good help and attending inspirational workshops and seminars is an excellent way to get motivated. That said, as for me, I hope this book empowers you to be your own guru and build your own skills for success.

Robert Kiyosaki

Robert Kiyosaki, author of the best-selling book *Rich Dad, Poor Dad*, highlights the difference between the traditional wisdom of seeking stability by working hard to climb a corporate ladder versus the strategic wisdom of building wealth by investing surplus with a view to achieving independence. Kiyosaki, the ultimate Investor, advises readers as to the importance of changing one's viewpoint on money and lifestyle in order to realize that spending your "fun money" every month might make you look and feel wealthy in the moment but dooms you to dependence upon employment for income.

Kiyosaki cautions people not to let fear force them into working harder than necessary for other peoples' goals, nor to let greed for status-reinforcing objects force them into an endless cycle of spending and debt. Essentially, he warns people against participating in "the rat race" and seeing its limited financial cycle as a goal. Instead, he teaches readers the wisdom of spending surplus funds on assets rather than liabilities.

Kiyosaki highlights the pitfalls inherent in many traditional viewpoints on financial planning and advises readers to instead view each dollar they own as a potential employee that could be put to work to earn more money, rather than spent. Further, Kiyosaki cautions against the emotional pitfalls of self-doubt, fear, laziness, arrogance, and guilt that can prevent investors from bucking the system in order to succeed.

Finally, Kiyosaki encourages readers to develop their financial independence far beyond the bounds of his book by reading and learning constantly in order to enjoy the world of investment and finance and see the benefits the "rich dad" mindset can have for their futures. I agree with this wise Investor's assertions. My work in this book simply expands upon his ideas and provides an efficient next step for those interested in seeking the financial knowledge that leads to true independence.

In my view, Kiyosaki and other similar gurus often belittle certain aspects of financial acumen that water down the focus of their "way." For instance, in his initial work, Kiyosaki emphasizes real estate and often discourages the idea of investing in high growth assets. I've seen how these small suggestions get blown out of proportion by the people interpreting such ideas as gospel.

Warren Buffet

Famed investor and entrepreneur Warren Buffet has been written about endlessly, although his own commentary on success with his Berkshire Hathaway conglomerate has been limited, in comparison. When asked his advice on investing, he tends to preach a conservative gospel most typical of the Saver. He tells people to simply invest in the S&P 500 index. Buffet's advice regarding investing leans not toward what is new and up-to-date but evergreen industries whose technology changes little over time. During the technology-based "New Economy" around the turn of the century, Buffet was quoted

> *The awake share a common world, but the asleep turn aside into private worlds*
>
> HERACLITUS

as saying, "We have embraced the 21st Century by entering cutting-edge industries such as brick, carpet, insulation, and paint. Try to control your excitement." His interest in such "boring" industries tends to help him avoid the volatility found in cutthroat, competitive, high-tech investments. At the same time, much of Buffet's wealth has been made through investments in private holdings, but he does not advise amateurs to delve into this realm.

He encourages frugality, noting, "If you buy things you don't need, soon you'll have to sell things you need." With just such a strategy in mind,

Buffet has asserted: "Simplicity is a supremely pious and boring thing that can be extremely beautiful." With the patience of a true Saver, he insists you should never invest in a stock unless you're interested in holding it for ten years, as only long-term investments ensure earning.

A big fan of regulated monopolies, Buffet asserts that such companies are key to bringing about positive change. After all, their existence is protected by the government because of their importance to society. In this, he asserts his strong belief in leveraging his assets for the less fortunate, showing himself to have a multi-faceted investment personality if ever there was one. Because Buffet is one of the world's most successful investors, it is tempting to view him not as a Saver but an Investor Financial Nature. At the same time, his career has put a strong emphasis on delegating (a strength exclusive to the Lever) and frugality (primarily strengths of the Earner and Saver). He has written extensively about the importance of donating and economic leadership (strengths of the Giver). As he has never taken my Financial Personality Assessment, I can only speculate as to Buffet's Nature, but I can say with confidence that with his even-tempered, long-term mindset, he is definitely not a Taker or Spender.

Larry Winget

Larry Winget is a pull-no-punches author and reality show star who wrote a hard-hitting book called, *You're Broke Because You Want to Be: How to Stop Getting By and Start Getting Ahead*. On his reality show, Big Spender, Winget ambushes debtors with extravagant lifestyles in the middle of a spending spree and forces them to take a hard look at their finances. Eventually, he provides a road map to repairing the mess they've made of their financial lives. Emotionally *reactive* to the core, Winget is a great example of the Taker Financial Nature in action.

Winget is no stock picker or investment guru. In fact, he advocates hiring such people to make the specific investment decisions necessary in any long-term financial plan. He is more like a financial planner crossed with a football coach. In fact, by his own admission, Winget is not a "put-an-arm-around-you-and-tell-you-everything-is-going-to-be-all-right kind of guy." His style is confrontational and demanding. At the same time, he doesn't advocate living the life of a pauper to pay off all debt in order to build some utopian, debt-free future, as Dave Ramsey does.

Winget disagrees with conservative voices who suggest money should be hoarded and saved for your inheritance, even as he channels the frugality of such individuals in his reprimands to spendthrift clients. Winget's strict, confrontational nature as a financial advisor is paired with a big heart in the sense that he believes life is meant to be lived today and money to be enjoyed … within reason. Winget asserts that **time** is best spent doing fun things with loved ones, but those things cost money to do. With this in mind, he sets about fixing what's wrong in order to get clients back to the business of living as soon as possible.

In my wheel diagram, Winget's *reactive* State as a Taker is right next to Orman's *feeling* State as a Spender, but he exhibits none of her touchy-feely communication style. In fact, the stark difference between these two individuals is a great example of the variety to be found among the highly emotional Natures of Taker and Spender.

All things come into being
by conflict of opposites

HERACLITUS

Leverage is Your Friend

Next, I'm going to take you deep inside a boots-on-the-ground situation of financial planning where I helped someone deep in debt reduce his financial stress not by getting a second job or living a monk-like existence but simply by using the system of Financial Levels, States, and Natures to achieve the leverage he needed to resume a peaceful, financially responsible lifestyle. Before we get into the nitty-gritty, though, let's review both the concept of leverage and the consequences experienced by those with a lack of leverage.

In the top three Financial Levels (Productive, Deductive, and Inductive) you'll notice that investment of surplus money plays a big role. Such investment is key to launching individuals (and institutions, companies, etc.) past the point of Proficiency and into the second-income-producing Levels. Investment is a complex subject, and I can't address every detail in this book, but I can talk here about the most essential aspect of it, which is leverage.

Bad Lending

The world's most wealthy people always owe something to somebody. Ironically, the world's poorest people also tend to be mired in debt. The difference between rich and poor isn't the amount of debt they carry but what that debt costs them. Exorbitant interest rates make debt a cinder block you have to drag around with you that only gets heavier with time. For instance, you've heard of "payday loans," right? That's where you have a job, so you expect a payday coming up in a week or so, but you need the money now.

Lending institutions offering payday loans provide the opportunity to borrow money immediately, for a short term, at very high interest. The Consumer Federation of America estimates that such loans (on anywhere from $200 to $2500) typically have finance charges of $25 on every $100 borrowed, compounded every two weeks. That's a 650% annual interest rate (APR). Such a borrower expects to pay the loan off quickly, so the expenditure feels like a necessary evil that can soon be neutralized. Hopefully that will be the case, but life is unpredictable.

If things don't go exactly as expected, this sky-high interest adds up over time, and the borrower ends up mired in debt that far supersedes his income. Payday loans are an extreme example of unhealthy borrowing and the kind of thing that gives debt a bad name. Obviously, this type of lending is something to be avoided at all costs. Most bank loans aren't this expensive, but they all charge an interest rate of some kind. Thus, borrowing money to get a surplus now means you'll have potentially quite a big deficit in the future. As we've discussed, **time** is a currency just like money, so taking out a loan with a high interest rate is gambling not just with money but also with your future. Very dangerous. That said, there is also a type of healthy debt.

Good Lending

What if you could take out a loan with 0% interest? That means you can take as long as you wish to pay it off because carrying that loan has no penalty.

Getting a loan for nothing is almost like getting free money. You still have to pay it back, but if no interest accrues, you can schedule a small amount to be automatically paid out of your bank account toward the debt each month, which (as long as you're gainfully employed) won't significantly affect your lifestyle, and you can basically forget about it. Of course, banks don't offer 0% interest loans. They'd go out of business! But you can use something called leverage to simulate a low- or no-interest loan.

As you know, when you borrow money, you have to pay interest on that loan. That's because your debtor has made an investment in you. Here's a simple example: if Jim's sister Jessica loans him $100 at 10% interest accrued weekly, she gets ten dollars in interest payments every week, as long as Jim still owes that $100. If Jim still owes the money in two and a half months, Jessica will have made back her investment and will start making a profit—all without doing any work whatsoever.

On the other hand, if Jim pays the loan off at $10 per week toward the principle, plus the interest he owes, then:

> ➤ *At week one, he'll pay $10 toward the principle and $10 in interest for a total of $20.*

> ➤ *At week two, he'll only owe $90 and pay $10 toward the principle and $9 in interest.*

> ➤ *At week three, he'll owe $80 and pay $10 toward the principle and $8 in interest.*

> ➤ *And so forth, all the way until he has paid off the loan in eight weeks' time.*

In this scenario, sister Jessica invests $100 over the course of eight weeks and receives her money back plus $55 in total interest payments. It might seem like eight weeks is a lot of time to spend to make just $55 dollars, but remember she did absolutely no work for that money. Imagine if she made loans to lots of people at the same rate; she'd bring in quite a haul, and all without lifting a finger. Here, Jessica is functioning (and profiting) like a bank.

When you work hard for your money, you're spending **energy** and **time** currencies to earn it. There is certainly nothing wrong with hard work, but the human ability to work and the hours we have to do it are limited, so only making money from your labor limits your potential income. On the other hand, when you invest surplus money like Jessica, dividends accrue without you spending any **time** or **health** currencies to get them. This brings us back to leveraging.

Learning about Leveraging

When you leverage, you borrow money from one entity (which results in a loss when you pay interest on the debt) but you also invest money with someone else (which results in a gain when you receive dividends from the investment). Quite simply, if the gain is greater than the loss, it results in an overall profit for you. If the loss and gain are exactly the same, the situation is neutral, which is also beneficial because that means you've borrowed money in such a way that the interest was exactly paid by your investment, meaning you averaged 0% interest for the loan, out of pocket. Let's take a look at Jim's situation again.

He borrowed $100 from his sister. But why did he do it? He needed that money to buy a lawn mower so he could start a business. With his lawn-mowing business, Jim made $40 per week, so the payments he had to make to Jessica (ranging from $20 to $11 per week over eight weeks) were still less than his profits. After eight weeks of hard work, he paid off his debt and enjoyed 100% profit from his business after that. Well done, Jim!

In this scenario, Jessica made $55 over eight weeks just from loaning Jim money. Meanwhile, Jim made $165 over the same time, but he had to work hard for it. Here's another way Jim could have approached the situation: he could simply rent out the lawn mower to another kid who wants to make money. Let's say he rents his friend Sam the lawnmower at the fee of $12 per week. Sam now goes out and mows the lawns and brings in the $40 per week Jim would have received if he had done the work. Thus:

> *Sam earns $320 over eight weeks but pays $96 in lawn mower rental. His profit after eight weeks of hard work is $224. He has spent a lot of time and effort to earn it.*

> *Jim earns $96 over eight weeks by investing his asset in Sam, meanwhile he does nothing at all.*

> *Jessica earns $55 over eight weeks, also doing nothing at all.*

Everyone in this scenario has made a profit, but between the two people who didn't lift a finger, Jim did better than Jessica. That's because he leveraged his assets. He borrowed money while simultaneously making an investment that earned more than the interest on his loan. Jim was in debt for those eight weeks, but his debt actually brought him a profit because of the way he leveraged it by investing the **stuff** he bought with the borrowed money.

If you have the ability to take out a loan for a reasonably low interest rate, you can do the same thing. For instance, if a bank enables you to take out a home equity loan at 2.5% APR, meanwhile you have the same amount of money invested in the stock market, making 2.5% annually, you are earning from your investment exactly what you need to pay on your loan, otherwise known as "breaking even." As an example: if the loan is for $5000, you're paying

When I wrote the draft for this book, interest rates were quite low. During editing and design, the Federal Reserve raised rates significantly. Rather than end up in a perpetual state of editing this section, keep in mind that home equity rates may be much higher by the time you read this. It's equally true that they may be back at 2.5% again. Who knows. Stocks as a result of changing interest rates also vary in price and yield. Regardless of changing rates, the example contains an important principle.

As we say in the business, past performance is not an indicator of future success, but it does help illustrate the principles needed to navigate in an uncertain world.

$125 annually for it (at 2.5%). But if you have $5000 invested in something else that brings in 2.5%, you're making $125 from that. In this situation, I recommend setting up autopay on the loan in such a way that the loan payment is drawn straight from your investment account, and you will experience what amounts to a 0% interest loan. That means you now have $5000 to spend on whatever you want, and you can pay it off at your leisure (since the interest on your loan is being paid off by the dividend on your investment).

You aren't necessarily at the Deductive Level here, but you might be. (At the Deductive Level, your investment accounts are set up to autopay not just this new debt, but all your regular debts and bills. This can only work if you're receiving enough in dividends from your investments and income to do so. The key to getting to this Level is wise investing, for which you'll probably want to see a financial planner or other investment professional.)

Making the Leap from Proficiency to Productivity

Now, you may ask: "If I have $5000 to invest in the stock market, why would I need to take out a $5000 loan in the first place? I could spend the $5000 and remain debt free."

This question represents a common misunderstanding about debt: that it is always bad. Let's look again at the Financial Levels. At the state of Proficiency, you begin to see a surplus in your bank account. Even if the surplus is small, if you resist the temptation to spend it and instead invest it in an interest-bearing account of some kind, it begins to accrue, and the interest does, too. You have thus lifted yourself up to the Productive Level. Over time, you may end up with a $5000 investment. If it's regularly earning 2.5% dividends, you are in the situation described above.

Perhaps at this point, you realize you need $5000 for some dental work. Sure, you could take the money out of your investment account, in which case you would avoid going into debt but would also no longer have an interest-earning investment. You'd plummet from the Productive state back down to Proficient, due to a lack of invested capital. This assumes you're still earning a surplus. If your career has taken a turn for the worse and you no longer enjoy surplus income, then you will instead plummet all the way down to Efficiency. Having investments is the crucial thing that keeps you from this downward trajectory.

The reason you don't want to drop a level is because if you keep that $5000 in the account, it will keep on earning interest for you even after your dental work is paid for. But as soon as you withdraw and spend the money, you lose all the potential interest income it would have earned in subsequent years, so, in the long run, the expenditure would cost you a lot more than $5000. For this reason, it makes more sense to actually take on debt as long as the interest on the debt is equal to or less than the interest you're earning on your investment. This way, the interest on the debt is paid by the investment, then, over time, you'll pay off the debt itself, and you'll still have money invested in a dividend-bearing account. That's why having the ability to invest and borrow in order to leverage is more important than staying out of debt.

To be economically self sufficient, you want to avoid going down in the Financial Levels. It does happen, and that's life, but whenever you can avoid doing so, that's your goal. When you have money invested, you don't want to pull it out, except to switch it over to a more lucrative investment. This is why once you get up to the Productive Level, where you have investments, it's entirely likely you will never drop below that level because your investments bring in passive income that gets you through the tough times.

Remember, in the lawn-mower-loan scenario, Jim went into debt to Jessica, but he made more money than she did and will continue to make money long after she does. That's because he borrowed money for an investment, leveraged that debt by loaning his asset to Sam, and kept the investment for future profits. For Jim, debt was good. If Jessica hadn't been there with her initial loan, though, Jim wouldn't have been able to engage in leveraging. He would have ended up like Sam: renting his equipment from someone else, thus dooming himself to a life of working hard for every penny. In this scenario, Sam's profit would be limited by the **time** and energy currencies he has available, so he would have very little opportunity to gain surplus.

By the way, making money from leveraging doesn't imply laziness or a lack of industry. There is, in fact, no reason why Jim and Jessica couldn't both go out and do additional work-for-cash labor while also making passive incomes from their loans. This would ensure they have both primary and secondary incomes and immediately place them at the Productive Financial Level.

Complete Your Journey with a Leveraging Case Study

A t Shepard Financial, I was approached by George, a young man in love but also in real trouble. He had recently gotten married to Sally, but they put all the wedding and honeymoon expenses on various credit cards that charged, on average, 19% interest. Now, he had four maxed-out credit cards to deal with, totaling about $60,000. George also had a good job and $60,000 in the bank. George wasn't in desperate straits (yet) but knew that if he didn't deal with this debt the right way, he could have just set himself and his new spouse up for a real financial problem that would only get worse, year after year. Furthermore, this debt was already affecting George's credit rating in such a way that he feared he wouldn't be able to buy a home for many years to come. He wanted to know if he should:

> ➤ *Take the Dave Ramsey approach, which would be to spend his $60,000 to pay off the credit card with the lowest balance, then live with extreme frugality for several years until he was able to shuttle every penny of surplus income into paying off his four debts as soon as possible in order to live debt free.*

> *Take the Suze Orman approach of paying off
> the debt with the highest interest rate first, then
> gradually paying off the other debts, but without
> the same sense of urgency promoted by Ramsey.*

Luckily, in the midst of his confusion, George knew enough to take the advice of Kiyosaki, Robbins, and Winget in the sense that he consulted a financial planner (me) to get professional guidance on the matter. I advised him that neither Ramsey nor Orman's solutions involved the complex leveraging strategy he needed to put this hassle to bed. Here's what we did instead.

Step One

When George took the Financial Natures assessment, it became clear that he was a Saver. Savers like to be in a *relaxed* State with their money, but ever since the wedding, George had been using every bit of surplus cash to pay down the debt while watching the interest continue to accrue very quickly. Nothing could have been less relaxing than this, but he didn't know how to move forward in the wheel of Financial States ... not consciously, at least. He did have the good sense to *create* an appointment with a financial planner, however, so something in his intuition guided him correctly to the next State: *create*. At our meeting, I proceeded to help him *elevate* his understanding of the concept of leverage.

I told him that leveraging is dependent upon one's ability to borrow money as well as invest it, so, because George's bad credit rating would prevent him from borrowing more money in the future, fixing his credit rating (rather than eradicating his debt) was the first problem we needed to solve. Now, I know what you're thinking: Borrow more money? When he's already $60,000 in debt? But remember: Leveraging isn't about being debt free, it's about making trades that result in the lowest possible interest rate on your debt. Stay with me.

Credit cards and other types of revolving debt report to credit-rating agencies and are weighted very heavily in the scoring systems, but installment loans are treated differently. So, we first needed to clear George's credit rating problems by refinancing those credit cards from revolving loans (credit cards) into installment loans (bank loans). Because George did not own a home or any other collateral significant enough to enable him to take out a low-interest installment loan from his local bank, I suggested George take out an unsecured bank loan. The interest on the unsecured loan was no better than that on the credit cards: 19%. This transfer of the loan amount saved George no money whatsoever, but it served an important purpose. With the debt transferred to an installment loan, his credit cards reported the debt paid, and within thirty days, his credit rating jumped by almost 100 points. This initial "lateral" move was the key to the rest of the leveraging process.

The next step in the wheel of Financial States is *lead*. But how is a man so deeply in debt going to take leadership?

Step Two

Once George's credit score had improved, he became eligible to take out a home loan. Even though he carried a significant debt, his income and credit score were now such that he could still take out a secured loan. So, I directed George to go ahead and buy a $300,000 home at the best interest rate he could get, using $60,000 of savings as a 20% down payment. By putting 20% down on the home purchase, he avoided primary mortgage insurance (PMI). Sally, a Lever, immediately understood the value of investing in something that could later be used as collateral, but George's Saver nature balked at the idea of acquiring another debt. His wife and I urged him to trust us, so he did.

Having bought the house, George then had a heck of a lot of debt:

> ➤ *$60,000 at 19%*

> ➤ *$240,000 at 4%*

It's understandable that George next went through the *react* State by freaking out a little bit about going into so much debt. But I reassured him that if he learned my system, he'd be able to save a lot more than ever before, in the long run. Thus reassured, he got in touch with his feelings (*feel* Financial State) and entered the *think* State, preparing himself to learn more.

As you examine this strategy, notice that if George had used his $60,000 in savings to pay off a significant chunk of his debt, he would not have had the money for the down payment. Now, he *still* has a debt at 19% (and another one at 4%) but he also has a home, which is a valuable asset he didn't have before.

Step Three

Now that George owned a home, he could take out a home equity loan, which is a low-interest loan secured by the value of the home. In this case, the bank becomes a second lienholder on the home in exchange for loaning George the $60,000 he needs to pay off his installment debt.

Thus, that $60,000 debt (formerly at a 19% interest rate) became a home equity loan at just 4%. Also, George owns a home now, which he can both live in and use as an asset against any future loans he may need. He still has to pay off his $60,000 debt, but it is at a reasonable interest rate that isn't going to ramp up too high, too quickly. He has now improved his debt situation to:

- $60,000 at 4%

- $240,000 at 4%

- For a total of $300,000 at 4%

George was happy with his new numbers and finally entered the *relaxed* State where Savers love to be. But wait, there's more!

Step Four

The final step in our process is to take away George's stress and make his life fun and easy, again. We do this by *creating* a system that automates his payments toward these debts. (As you can see, we're going around the wheel of Financial States, once more.) Each automated payment will include a significant chunk toward the principal so that, over time, George will see a decrease in the amount he owes. In the meantime, the payments won't be so great that they impede his family's ability to enjoy life.

His payments being lower would also allow the two of them to increase their 401k contributions and lower their tax liability. Because I knew that retirement was being more than adequately funded, I suggested they pay off the rest of the high-interest-rate debt by taking out a 401k loan. Since the 401k loan on a home purchase is payable over 30 years, I suggested George and Sally consider using some of that money instead of cash to finance a portion of the down payment. Life is easier when we understand how to lower our expenses. Lower taxes, lower interest, lower fees, and lower premiums are all desirable, but a life where those things are all zero is never the objective.

George and Sally enjoyed a magical wedding. They didn't finance it so wisely and were paying for that mistake, but, as you can see, this is a fixable problem, especially when one consciously cycles through the Financial States and utilizes the concept of leverage. In the future, George and Sally will know better than to use credit cards for such massive expenses. And now that they own a home, they'll be able to take out a low-interest home equity loan next time a big expense like that arises. Since they are over-funding their retirement, it's okay to borrow against it.

Summing Up Part 6: Boots On The Ground

Just like George and Sally, you too can take advantage of the concept of leverage in order to handle your own financial problems or embark upon a new financial adventure. But, as you can see, there is a lot to learn when it comes to the nitty-gritty of manipulating currency in order to reduce the cost of debts and increase the value of assets. It is for this reason that I run Currency Camp, in Yarmouth, Maine. This is a learning opportunity that provides people with the down-to-Earth knowledge they need to take advantage of the principles in this book to become their own financial gurus.

Hopefully, this book has taught you how to know yourself and your loved ones better, value the various currencies in your life, and set specific, reasonable goals for the acquisition of those currencies. Money is only one currency, but perhaps the most difficult one to manage and fully understand. The principles in this book should have, by now, given you a good grounding in ways to improve every aspect of your life with an understanding of the currencies, Financial Natures, Financial Levels, and Financial States.

If you feel inspired to improve upon your ability to leverage debts against assets, I hope to see you for a session of Currency Camp. In any case, never stop learning, as understanding the wonderful world of currency is the key to enjoying your adventure through the financial wilderness.

No man ever steps in the same river twice, for it's not the same river and he's not the same man

HERACLITUS

Money and Happiness

Up to a point, Money can buy happiness, but happiness isn't that easy to quantify. For instance, various studies have shown that beyond a certain limit, earning more money doesn't make people happier. Other studies show that buying experiences rather than **stuff** leads to happier outcomes. Furthermore, studies on longevity and happiness often assume that the statistical fact that people live longer in some countries means their residents must be happier and more content than others. What all these studies miss is that their conclusions probably don't apply universally. Such relationships between wealth, happiness, and longevity might be right for some people and wrong for others. Would you be at all surprised if I told you that there are seven ways to be happy and one that really resonates with you?

My work over these many years has helped me see a pattern that you now have used over and over again in this book. So, when happiness was raised as a topic recently, I was intrigued enough to fly down to Costa Rica to UPEACE to attend a conference on global happiness. There, I discussed with others the fact that the measure of our success here on this planet is partly a function of pursuing happiness. We don't all pursue happiness the same way and certainly aren't always looking for the same experiences as we do so. In fact, pursuing happiness the same way, over and over, causes it to lose its effectiveness. Being happy is like chewing gum for too long. It loses its flavor. So, here's a quick little bonus piece on buying happiness.

The nature of the *reactor*/Taker, is that of looking for activities that are exciting. Often, Takers are most happy when things are on the edge. They enjoy a combination of passion and fun. The endorphins come from the rush of excitement.

The Spender/*feeler* is more likely to be happy when things are fun and funny. Too much work or excitement waters down or drowns out the good and happy feelings.

Earner/worker/*thinker* types are most often happy when experiencing the satisfaction of a job well done. For them, having solved a problem releases its own success hormones.

Saver/*relaxers* are often happiest when comfortably held in the arms of their favorite chair or hammock. For them, a bath or nap might be just the thing to turn a tough day into one with a happy ending.

Come on!
Let's go!

SYDNEY
MADISON
SHEPARD

The Investor/*creator* may seem to crave excitement, but this person's happiness comes in the flavor of joy. The enjoyment of being part of a creative process is a means to finding great happiness for these types. Creativity is not theirs alone, but alone, that state of creative flow is all that's needed.

The Lever/*uplifter* is happiest when things are easy. The absence of difficulty may not trigger some to be happy, but for this Nature, hard work is not a prerequisite to getting the uplifting feeling of happiness.

Giver/*leaders* often find happiness in outward expressions of their inner feelings. Passion is, above all, one of the keywords of this Nature. We would do well to be aware of how important it is for some very giving people to have outlets for their generosity.

So, there it is: the seven Natures lead to seven types of happiness. The number seven appears again, helping us to accept the way others perceive and pursue happiness in different ways. Opening ourselves up to the variety that life is trying to share with us is a great way to discover and rediscover ways to be happy. In the end, this is my wish for you: that you see all four currencies as a way to "buy" happiness and therefore fall in love with what they can do for you.

Index

About Tom Shepard

Tom Shepard has worked in finance for over 27 years. He both attended and taught at the Institute for Civic Leadership, and produced writings on the Seven Levels of Sustainable Nonprofits. Additionally, he taught personal finance and mathematics at Gould Academy, and is an avid speaker. Now, he leads Shepard FINANCIAL, a comprehensive financial planning and personalized investment management group, as well as Currency Camp, which offers financial advice to groups and individuals.

Shepard has been a guest on Dr. Lisa Belisle's "Dr. Lisa Radio Hour" and Debi Davis's "Mind Your Own Business."

In addition to his work in the finance world, Tom is an avid lacrosse player and skier. He lives with his family in Cumberland, Maine.

VISIT TOM AT

WWW.SHEPARD-FINANCIAL.COM

www.ingramcontent.com/pod-product-compliance
Lightning Source LLC
Chambersburg PA
CBHW071147130626
46553CB00004B/1557